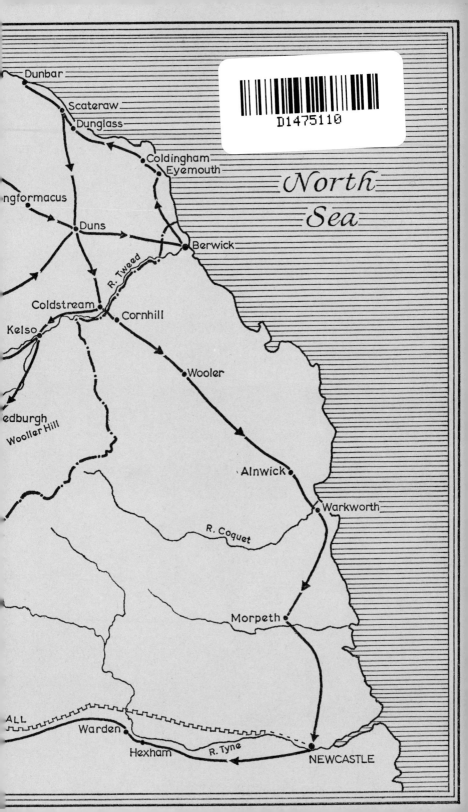

ROBERT BURNS'S TOUR OF THE BORDERS
5 MAY—1 JUNE 1787

ALSO BY RAYMOND LAMONT BROWN

History of St Mark's Church, Dewsbury, 1865–1965
A Book of Epitaphs
Doncaster Rural District: Official Guide
Clarinda
Sir Walter Scott's Letters on Demonology & Witchcraft
Robert Burns's Commonplace Book 1783–85
A Book of Superstitions
A Book of Proverbs
A Book of Witchcraft
A Second Book of Epitaphs
Charles Kirkpatrick Sharpe's Historical Account of the Belief of
Witchcraft in Scotland

Robert Burns's Tour
of the Borders
5 MAY—1 JUNE 1787

RAYMOND LAMONT BROWN

Deb.

Here is a fellow traveler for your spiritual wanderings.

Tom
1987

Rowman and Littlefield

© RAYMOND LAMONT BROWN 1972

ALL RIGHTS RESERVED

PUBLISHED BY ROWMAN AND LITTLEFIELD INC
87 ADAMS DRIVE, TOTOWA, NEW JERSEY 07512

ISBN 0 87471 123 1

PRINTED IN GREAT BRITAIN BY
THE ANCHOR PRESS LTD, AND
BOUND BY WM. BRENDON & SON LTD,
BOTH OF TIPTREE, ESSEX

Contents

Illustrations

Endpaper Map: Robert Burns's Tour of the Borders

Acknowledgments

No work of historical research is complete these days without a list of acknowledgments. Space however, proscribes the tabulation here of all those who have given assistance in making this book possible. I would, however, like to mention the following, who have given conspicuous help: The Librarian and staffs of the Northumberland County Library; the Carlisle Public Library; the Berwickshire County Library; Edinburgh University Library; East Lothian County Library; Central Public Library, Edinburgh; the Signet Library, Edinburgh, and my own local Libary at Berwick-upon-Tweed. I proffer my thanks also to the Estates Office, Alnwick Castle, the Town Clerk of Duns, the Royal Commission on the Ancient and Historical Monuments of Scotland, the Royal College of Surgeons, Edinburgh and the Ordnance Survey in Scotland.

The photographs have been acknowledged separately.

For my good friend and colleague
PROFESSOR TOSHIO NAMBA
of Nihon University, Tokyo
who has helped to promote
ROBERT BURNS
in Japan

Then let us pray that come it may,
  As come it will, for a' that,
That sense and worth o'er a' the earth,
  Shall bear the gree, and a' that:
For a' that, and a' that,
  It's coming yet, for a' that,
That man to man, the warld o'er
  Shall brithers be for a' that.

Sono tokino Kuruno wo minade inorō
Sono toki wa kitto kuruni chigainai
Sekai jūno hitobito ga rhyōshiki to kachi wo
Saikōno kokorono kate to suru hi
Yono nariyuki wo kaerimireba
Sono hiwa chikozuite iru
Sekai jūno hitobito ga
Kyōdai ni naru hiya.

INTRODUCTION

Robert Burns and his journals

Robert Burns is known to have kept a regular journal on two occasions only, and both are dated 1787: the first recounted his late summer visit to the Highlands, and the second his tour of the Borders. It should be noted that some scholars still refer to Robert Burns's *Second Commonplace Book 1787–90* as the 'Edinburgh Journal': the latter, however, was never a journal in the accepted sense.

Dr James Currie (1756–1805), Burns's first editor and major biographer, made some passing use of the Highland and Border journals: but what was alleged to be the complete text was first published by Allan Cunningham (1784–1842), a Scottish poet and man of letters, in his disastrously inaccurate eight volume *The Works of Robert Burns, with his Life* (1834); after being further quoted by John Gibson Lockhart (1794–1854), Sir Walter Scott's son-in-law, in his misleading and dishonest *Life of Robert Burns* (1828).

Some years before World War II the original of the Highland journal came to light once more, but it proved to be considerably briefer than Cunningham's printed text. The late J. C. Ewing, who edited this journal in facsimile in 1927, believed that the additions were made by Burns, in a recension—now lost—of his original penciled notes. Professor F. B. Snyder, however, in his *Life of Robert Burns** regarded Cunningham as the author of the revisions. In the absence of Burns's own enlarged manuscript, and of any proof that such a work existed, Snyder's conclusion seems to be the most likely: but this academic puzzle remains.

With this editorial tampering in mind and the obvious suspicion with which all scholars must treat the biographical work of Currie, Cunningham and Lockhart, Robert Burns's

---

*New York, 1932 p. 224, p. 254 n.

[2]

Border journal remains as Cunningham published it, for examination of the holograph text reveals neither rewriting nor expansion. Nevertheless, it should be noted that the academically slipshod Cunningham omitted several hundred words, and at the close gives three entries which are not now—and apparently never were—with the rest of the journal. The main text, moreover, is followed by fourteen pages of miscellaneous memoranda, some of which, like the omitted pages of the diary itself, have biographical significance.

The original journal of the tour traced

Robert Burns's original holograph manuscript of his Border tour is still in the hands of the Murray family, who own the publishing house of John Murray Ltd, of Albemarle Street, London. The manuscript had been bequeathed in 1873 to the late Lt.-Col Sir John Murray's grandfather by James Robert Hope (known after 1853 as Hope-Scott), who had married as his first wife Charlotte Lockhart, a granddaughter of Sir Walter Scott. Apparently the manuscript had been given (sometime before 1854) to James Robert Hope's father, General the Hon. Sir Alexander Hope of Rankeillour and Luffness, by John Gibson Lockhart. It is not clear how Lockhart first acquired this holograph manuscript, as no records, for instance at Abbotsford, are extant to show its receipt. The manuscript however, was in Burns's possession at his death and was collected by John Syme as background research material for Currie's life of Burns. What happened to the manuscript after Currie's death in 1805 is uncertain. There is certainly no evidence to suggest that Lockhart bought the manuscript.

Today the journal comprises fifty-seven octavo pages, all written in ink except for a few of the miscellaneous notes at the end. Nine leaves at the commencement of the text have been torn out (Sir John Murray always averred that this was done by someone to whom his grandfather rashly lent the book.) Initial letters remaining on the torn stubs of the leaves indicate that they contained unidentifiable verse, which must have totalled around ninety to one hundred lines. This verse could, of course, have been some of Burns's bawdy lines which shocked a tender Victorian's righteousness.

Background to the Border tour

There were two main reasons which urged Burns to undertake his Border tour. One he set out in his letter of 22 March 1787 to his frequent correspondent Mrs Frances Anna Wallace Dunlop of Dunlop (1730–1815):

> I have no greater, no dearer aim than to have it in my power, unplagu'd with the routine of business, for which Heaven knows I am unfit enough, to make leisurely pilgrimages through Caledonia; to sit on the fields of her battles; to wander on the romantic banks of her rivers; and to muse by the stately tower or venerable ruins, once the honored abodes of her heroes . . .*

The second reason arose out of an offer made to Burns by Patrick Miller (1731–1815), who had in 1785 purchased the estate of Dalswinton, on the River Nith, near Dumfries. A man of some means, Miller admired Burns's work, sent him an anonymous gift of ten guineas and offered him the lease of a farm on his estate.

Burns chose as his travelling companion a law student called Robert Ainslie. Born in 1766, Ainslie was the son of the land-steward of Lord Douglas's Berwickshire estates: and when Burns met him in 1787 he was a law student in the Edinburgh office of Samuel Mitchelson. Of carefree disposition, with a zestful pleasure for wine, women and song, Ainslie

---

*James Currie, *The Works of Robert Burns,* 1800.

matched Burns's variable character. In a letter dated 23 July 1787, Burns thus wrote to Ainslie from Mauchline: 'There is one thing for which I set great store by you as a friend, and it is this—that I have not a friend upon earth, besides yourself, to whom I can talk nonsense without forfeiting some degree of his esteem.' During his later years Ainslie turned religious and often played down his debauched days with Burns. He died in 1838.

For his touring Burns bought in Edinburgh a mare for 'over £4 sterling', which he nicknamed 'Jenny Geddes'. This was the name which Scottish tradition has given to the woman who, on 23 August 1637, in St Giles Cathedral, Edinburgh, is said to have thrown a stool at the Bishop of Edinburgh, who was trying to force into use in the Scottish Church *The Book of Common Prayer* on the authority of Charles I. Burns described the horse in some detail in his letter to William Nicol.*

In his twenty-eight years Burns had experienced much trial and tribulation. While his period in Edinburgh had left him elated, he was ready for the break which the Border tour was to give him. For a picture of how Burns appeared to others in the year of his Border tour, we have the three portraits and one silhouette extant of him at this time and two contemporary word pictures. One is by Dugald Stewart (1753–1828), Professor of Moral Philosophy at Edinburgh and the other is by Sir Walter Scott. Stewart's picture of Burns appears in Currie's edition of *The Works of Robert Burns* (1800):

> The first time I saw Robert Burns, was on 23d of October 1786, when he dined at my house in Ayrshire . . . [*near Catrine, a village within two miles of Mauchline. The meeting was described by Burns in the 'Lines on meeting with Lord Daer'.*] His manners were then, as they continued ever afterwards, simple, manly, and independent; strongly expressive of conscious genius and worth; but without anything that indicated forwardness,

---

* See Appendix I.

Burns's career up to the Border Tour

1759 Burns born at Alloway, near Ayr, 25 January.
      I was born a very poor man's son. My father was
      gardener to a worthy gentleman of small estate. Had
      he continued in that station, I must have marched off
      to be one of the little underlings about a farm-house;
      but it was his dearest wish and prayer to have it in
      his power to keep his children under his own eye till
      they could discern between good and evil.

1766 Burns family tenants of Mount Oliphant, a farm near
      Ayr (May).

1773 Burns writes his first poem—*O, once I lov'd a bonnie lass.*

1775 Spends the summer at a school in Kirkoswald to learn
      surveying &c.

1777 The Burnses move to Lochlea, in Tarbolton (May).

1780 Burns active in founding a Bachelor's Debating Club at
      Tarbolton (November).

1781–2 Resides in Irvine to learn flax-dressing.
      During this period reads the *Poems* of Robert Fergusson
      (1750–74) and is excited to emulation.

1783 Begins his first *Commonplace Book** (April)

1784 Burns's father dies at Lochlea, a poor man (13 February).
      With his brother Gilbert, leases Mossgiel, near Mauchline,
      from Gavin Hamilton. Meets Jean Armour at a 'penny
      dance' in Mauchline (April).
      Birth of Burns's first illegitimate child, Betty (November).
          When my father died, my brother and I took a
          neighbouring farm. But the first year from unfortun-
          ately buying bad seed, the second from a late harvest,
          we lost half our crops.
          Then came a most melancholy affair with Jean
          Armour which I cannot yet bear to reflect on. I gave up
          my part of the farm to my brother and made what
          little preparation was in my power for Jamaica.

1786 By April Burns had given Jean Armour a written acknow-
      ledgement of marriage, and learnt that Jean, at her father's
      wish, had agreed to the mutilation of his 'paper'.
      Poems, chiefly in the Scottish Dialect published at Kil-
      marnock (31 July).

1786–88 Burns in Edinburgh.
      Edinburgh edition of his *Poems*, 'printed for the Author
      and sold by William Creech'.

---

* *Robert Burns's Commonplace Book 1783–85,* ed. Raymond Lamont
Brown, Wakefield, Yorks. 1969.

arrogance, or vanity. He took his share in conversation, but not more than belonged to him; and listened with apparent attention and deference, on subjects where his want of education deprived him of the means of information. If there had been a little more of gentleness and accommodation in his temper, he would, I think, have been still more interesting; but he had been accustomed to give law in the circle of his ordinary acquaintance, and his dread of anything approaching to meanness or servility, rendered his manner somewhat decided and hard.—Nothing perhaps was more remarkable among his various attainments, than the fluency, and precision, and originality of his language, when he spoke in company; more particularly as he aimed at purity in his turn of expression, and avoided more successfully than most Scotchmen, the peculiarities of Scottish phraseology. . . .

The attentions he received during his stay [*at Edinburgh*] from all ranks and descriptions of persons, were such as would have turned any head but his own. I cannot say that I could perceive any unfavourable effect which they left on his mind. He retained the same simplicity of manners and appearance which had struck me so forcibly when I first saw him in the country; nor did he seem to feel any additional self-importance from the number and rank of his new acquaintance. His dress was perfectly suited to his station, plain and unpretending, with a sufficient attention to neatness. If I recollect right, he always wore boots; and, when on more than usual ceremony, buck-skin breeches . . . He was passionately fond of the beauties of nature . . .

The idea which his conversation conveyed of the powers of his mind, exceeded, if possible, that which is suggested by his writings. Among the poets whom I have happened to know, I have been struck, in more than one instance, with the unaccountable disparity between their general talents, and the occasional inspirations of their more favoured moments. But all the faculties of Burns's mind were, as far as I could judge, equally vigorous; and his predilection for poetry, was rather the result of his own enthusiastic and impassioned temper, than of a genius exclusively adapted to that species of composition. From his conversation I should have pronounced him to be fitted to excel in whatever walk of ambition he had chosen to exert his abilities.

Among the subjects on which he was accustomed to dwell, the characters of the individuals with whom he happened to meet was plainly a favourite one. The remarks he made on them were always shrewd and pointed, though frequently inclining too much to sarcasm. His praise of those he loved was sometimes indiscriminate and extravagant; but this, I suspect, proceeded rather from the caprice and humour of the moment, than from the effects of attachment in blinding his judgment. His wit was ready, and always impressed with the marks of vigorous understanding; but, to my taste, not often pleasing or happy. His attempts at epigram in his printed works, are the only performances perhaps, that he has produced, totally unworthy of his genius.

Sir Walter Scott's assessment of him during 1786–87 appeared in Lockhart's *Life of Robert Burns* (1828):

His person was strong and robust; his manners rustic, not clownish; a sort of dignified plainness and simplicity, which received part of its effect, perhaps, from one's knowledge of his extraordinary talents. His features are represented in Mr Nasmyth's picture, but to me it conveys the idea, that they are diminished, as if seen in perspective. I think his countenance was more massive than it looks in any of the portraits. I would have taken the poet, had I not known what he was, for a very sagacious country farmer of the old Scotch school, i.e. none of your modern agriculturists, who keep labourers for their drudgery, but the *douce gudeman* [*prudent and respectable head of the house*] who held his own plough. There was a strong expression of sense and shrewdness in all his lineaments; the eye alone, I think, indicated the poetical character and temperament. It was large, and of a dark cast, which glowed (I say literally *glowed*) when he spoke with feeling or interest. I never saw such another eye in a human head, though I have seen the most distinguished men of my time. His conversation expressed perfect self-confidence, without the slightest presumption. Among the men who were the most learned of their time and country, he expressed himself with perfect firmness, but without the least intrusive forwardness; and when he differed in opinion, he did not hesitate to express it firmly, yet at the same time with modesty.

Scott's opinion was based on only one meeting with Burns. At the time Scott was fifteen years old and a very junior guest at a literary meeting at the house of Professor Adam Ferguson (1723–1816), where Burns was being lionised by 'literary people . . . with the gentry of the west country'.

Some four years after his Border tour it looked as if Burns might again visit the Borders. At that time he was resident at Ellisland, Dumfries. David Stewart Erskine, 11th Earl of Buchan (1742–1829), who delighted to pose as a patron of literature, arranged for a celebration of the poet James Thomson's birthday at Ednam, near Kelso. Amongst those invited to this celebration was Burns: Burns, however, was not able to attend. Incidentally the Thomson ceremony turned out to be a complete disaster. The bust of Thomson to be crowned at the height of the ceremony was smashed in a drunken frolic before its erection, and the Earl had to content himself with laying a wreath of bay leaves on a volume of Thomson's poems.

What general topics concerning the Borderer's way of life would Burns, as a 'chiel takin' notes', be most likely to record mentally? In the first place, perhaps, living standards. Scots and Northumbrians living in the Borders at the time of Burns's visit, enjoyed a much better standard of living than those say in Argyllshire and the north and west. Even so, their families, like those of all other agricultural workers in Scotland, were held in chronic bondage to unrewarding labour. This was mainly because such early medieval techniques as the run-rig system of husbandry were followed with little adaptation,

thus the soil yielded poor results. Burns notes in his journal
that the soil of the Merse was far better than that of his native
country; even so he must have noticed the same hint of
malnutrition which sapped his relatives' strength and
burdened their lives.

As may be seen in the *Statistical Account of Scotland* (1799),
by 1787 the quality of Border stock had greatly improved,
partly as a result of enclosure by dykes, which enabled owners
to keep their herds separate from those of other people.
But much better winter feeding became available as more
turnips and grasses were grown. In the main however, farm
implements were slow to change during the eighteenth century;
but the hardy Borderers did have that spark of native genius
which led them to experiment. For instance, a Berwickshire
man James Small invented a swing plough in 1764. For the
first time after this one ploughman could manipulate the
plough alone with one pair of horses. Again, as Burns records,
Andrew Meikle in 1784 produced a most important innovation,
the power-driven threshing machine.

Traditional designs of domestic architecture and sanitary
conditions did not help the Borderer's environment. Wherever
Burns travelled he would see the familiar one-roomed cottages,
built of loose stones and clay. In his *The Autobiography of a
Working Man* (1848), Alexander Somerville describes the
dwelling, 'one of a row of sheds' in Berwickshire in which his
parents lived for a time with their eight children. It was:

> . . . about twelve feet by fourteen, and not so high in the
> walls as will allow a man to get in without stooping.
> That place without ceiling or anything beneath the bare
> tiles of roof; with no floor save the common clay; without
> a cupboard or recess of any kind; with no grate but the
> iron bars which the tenants carried to it, built up and took
> away when they left it; with no partition of any kind save
> what the beds made; with no window save four small
> panes at one side—it was this house, still a hind's house at
> Springfield, for which, to obtain leave to live in, my mother
> sheared the harvest and carried the stacks.

Even the windows were not necessarily part of the fittings provided—Somerville explains how his parents 'had a window consisting of one small pane of glass, and when they moved from one house to another in different parts of Berwickshire in different years they carried this window with them:

Recounting his visit to Roxburghshire Burns noted how rents tended to be low in the Borders; which was just as well, as labourers were earning approximately £3.00 (worth around £24.00 to £30.00 in terms of modern spending value) per year by 1787. Thus although food was cheap, standards of life remained miserable. The landowners, by and large were as hard put to maintain a reasonable comfort for their families, since much of their rent was paid in kind, and being perpetually short of cash, they had nothing to invest and no means of undertaking improvements. In every century before the middle of the nineteenth, Border society was dominated by these landowners. Although at the highest level their leadership might be deflected and guided by the overriding power of the English crown, or influenced and occasionally challenged by the high claims of the Kirk, on the local scene the power of the laird who gave the lease and took the rent was absolute.

Political and religious power was not invested in the common people of the Borders. Able to enjoy the rights of heritor, paternal lordship and nomination of the local clergy, the Border landowners were also the politico-religious leaders in 1787. In politics the Border folk who had the vote were manifestly Whig because of their dissenting character, but there were a few pockets of vociferous Tory landowners. In religion, Calvinism was supreme with a high degree of superstition and religious intolerance and hypocracy. Education was of a somewhat primitive nature: charity and church schools were to be found throughout the Borders with a few grammar schools, but by and large Borderers were unlettered. Yet the fostering of folk rhymes and ballads by word of mouth was very popular.

In the south-east Borders agriculture was the predominant occupation with a scattering of household industries, textiles, papermaking, shipbuilding, smuggling, poaching and fishing. By and large goods in the Borders were transported by horseback; wheeled traffic hereabouts was not common even in Burns's time. And the going was slow: one carrier working the forty miles between Selkirk and Edinburgh took two weeks to complete his return journey; indeed this carter found that he made the best progress by wading his horses along the bed of the Gala river, a safer and easier route than was afforded by the main roads. It was certainly quicker to ship goods by sea from Edinburgh to Berwick than to trust to the roads. By the last quarter of the eighteenth century, the post linking certain Border towns to Edinburgh was put on an official basis. In 1787 Berwick, Kelso, Selkirk, Hawick, Jedburgh and so on were all linked with each other and the capital by post riders.

The general landscape of the Borders in Burns's day was more heavily wooded than it is today and the moorland and 'plantations' more encroaching.

What the journal reveals

The Robert Burns who appears in the pages of this journal is less of a solid figure than the tenant farmer poet who cuts a dash in his other prose works. The Border journal, however, does show the Burns of rustic genius who fills his pages with materials for future exotic reveries, but who seems to have suffered increasing boredom from the heavy farmers, and saw through the pretensions of the patronising gentry. Perhaps the manuscript shows too much self-consciousness to be a great journal, but it is essential to Burns scholars for it adds much to the data which gives Burns a chance to speak for himself without the intervention of a censorious or moralising biographer or editor.

In my edition of *Robert Burns's Commonplace Book,* I averred that Burns had the necessary talent to produce a novel, essays, a play, or even a dossier of competent criticism. In the light of research done for this edition of the journal, my belief, in Burns's prose capabilities is no less. In this journal Burns shows a keen eye for characterisation and domestic atmosphere, a development of which could have made him rival and certainly outclass in northern sales, the works of such as Tobias Smollett, Henry Fielding and Laurence Sterne among others.

Strangely enough Burns did not catch the spirit of the ancient balladists which lingered at the monastic houses of Kelso, Jedburgh, Dryburgh and Melrose. Burns wrote nothing on them—they had to wait for Sir Walter Scott for literary immortality. Although Burns shows a farmer's keen eye for the land, a poet's for the places celebrated in song, and a critic's for human character, he was neither interested in the history nor romantic about the 'scenery'. This may have been the reason why he seems to have missed so much on his tour: he makes no mention for instance, of the battlefields of Pinkie and Flodden, even after expressing an interest in the subject to Mrs Dunlop.

All in all, the tour was something of a triumphant progress, his fame having preceded him down the post roads. In the main he would find the fellowship among the Border lairds and merchants far more satisfying than that he had encountered among the affected society of Edinburgh. But for Burns this tour was a stimulus; it increased his unfailing interest in Scots speech and folk song and stirred him to do better as a poet.

THE JOURNAL OF THE
BORDER TOUR

Annotated Transcription

[*The tour began at Edinburgh on 5 May 1787 and Burns proceeded by way of Haddington, Gifford and Longformacus.*]

May 6th

Left Edinr.—Lammermuir hills miserably dreary but at times very picturesque—Lanton edge a glorious view of the Merse¹—reach Berrywell²—Old Mr. Ainslie³ an uncommon character—his hobbies Agriculture natural philosophy & politics—In the first he is unexceptionably the clearest-headed, best-informed man I ever met with; in the other two, very intelligent—As a Man of business he has uncommon merit, and by fairly deserving it has made a very decent independance—Mrs Ainslie⁴ an excellent, sensible, chearful, amiable old woman—Miss Ainslie⁵ an angel—her person a little of the embonpoint but handsome her face, particularly her eyes full of sweetness and good humour—she unites three qualities rarely to be found together, keen, solid penetration; sly, witting observation and remark; and the gentlest, most unaffected female Modesty—Douglas⁶ a clever, fine, promising young fellow—The family meeting with their brother, my compagnion [*sic*] de voyage, very charming, particularly the sister—

The whole family remarkably attached to their menials—Mrs A[*inslie*]—full of stories of the sagacity & sense of the little girl in the kitchen—Mr A[*inslie*]—high in the praises of an African,⁷ his house servant—All his people old in his service—Douglas's old Nurse came to Berry-well yesterday to [tell–*deleted*] remind them of its being Douglas's birth day—

A Mr Dudgeon,⁸ a Poet at times, a worthy, remarkable character—[a good deal of–*deleted*] natural penetration, a great deal of information, some genius, and extreme Modesty—

[16]

Sunday—went to church at Dunse[9]—Dr. Bowmaker[10] a man of strong lungs and pretty judicious remark; but ill skilled in propriety, and altogether unconscious of his want of it[11]—

Monday [*7 May*]—Coldstream[12]—went over to England— Cornhill[13]—glorious river Tweed—clear & majestic—fine bridge[14]—dine at Coldm. with Mr. Ainslie & Mr Foreman[15] —beat Mr F[*oreman*]—in a dispute about Voltaire[16]—tea at Len[n]el house with Mr Brydon[17]—Mr Brydon a man of quite ordinary natural abilities, ingenious but not deep, chearful but not witty, a most excellent heart, kind, joyous & benevolent but a good deal of the French indiscriminate complaisance— from his situation past & present an admirer of every thing that bears a splendid title or possesses a large estate—Mrs Brydon a most elegant woman in her person and manners, the tones of her voice remarkably sweet—My reception from Mr. & Mrs. Brydon extremely flattering—Sleep at Coldstream—

Tuesday [*8 May*]—breakfast at Kelso[18]—charming situation of Kelso—fine bridge over Tweed[19]—enchanting views & prospects on both sides of the river, particularly the Scotch side; introduced to Mr Scot[20] of the royal bank—an excellent modest fellow—visit Roxburgh Palace[21]—fine situation of it —ruins of Roxburgh castle—a holly bush growing where James 2d of Scotland was accidently killed by the bursting of a cannon—a small old religious ruin[22] and a fine old garden planted by the religious, rooted out and destroyed by an English hottentot, a Maitre d'hotel of the Duke's, a Mr. Cole, climate & soil of Berwick shire & even Roxburgh shire superiour to Ayrshire—bad roads—turnip & sheep husbandry their great improvements—Mr. Mcdowall at Caverton[23] mill a friend of Mr. Ainslie's, with whom I dined, today, sold his sheep, ewe & lamb together, at two guineas a piece—wash their sheep before shearing—7 or 8 lb of washen wool in a fleece—low markets, consequently low rents—fine lands not above 16 sh Scots acre—Magnificence of Farmers & farm houses—came up Teviot & up Jed to Jedburgh[24] to lie, & so wish myself goodnight.

Wedensday [9 May]

Breakfast with Mr. Fair[25] in Jedburgh a blind man but the
first man of business as a Writer[26] in town—a squabble
between Mrs F[*air*], a craz'd talkative Slattern and a sister of
hers an old maid, respecting a relief Minister—Miss gives
Madam the lie, & Madam by way of revenge upbraids her that
she laid snares to entangle the said minister, then a widower,
in the net of matrimony—go about two miles out of Jedburgh
to a roup of [*grass*] Parks[27]—meet a polite soldier-like gentleman, a Captn. Rutherford who had been many years thro the
wilds of America, a prisoner among the Indians—Charming,
romantic situation, of Jedburgh, with gardens, orchards, &c.
intermingled among the houses—fine old ruins, a once
magnificent Cathedral [and strong castle-*deleted*]—All the
towns here have the appearance of old, rude grandeur; but
extremely idle—Jed a fine romantic little river—

Dine with Captn. Rutherford. The Captn. a specious polite
fellow, very fond of money in his farming way, but showed a
particular respect to My Bardship—his lady exactly a proper
matrimonial second part for him—Miss Rutherford a beautiful girl, but too far gone woman to expose so much of so fine a
swelling bosom—her face tho' very fine rather inanimately
heavy—return to Jedburgh—walk up Jed with some ladies to
be shown Love-lane & Black-burn two fairy scenes—introduced to Mr Potts,[30] Writer, a very clever fellow; & Mr
Somerville[31] the clergyman of the place, a man & a gentleman,
but sadly addicted to punning—The walking Partie of ladies—
Mrs F[*air*] & Miss Lookup her sister before-mentioned.
N.B. these two appear still more comfortably ugly & stupid,
and bore me most shockingly—[The-*deleted*] Two Miss Fairs,
tolerably agreable but too much of the Mother's half-ell[32]
[features-*deleted*] mouth & hag-like features—Miss Hope,[33]
a tolerably pretty girl, fond of laughing & fun—Miss Lindsay[34]
a good-humor'd amiable girl; rather short et embonpoint,
but handsome and extremely graceful—beautiful hazle eyes
full of spirit & sparkling with delicious moisture—an engaging
face & manner, un tout ensemble that speaks her of the first

order of female minds—her sister, a bonie, strappan, rosy, sonsie lass[35]—Shake myself loose, after several unsuccessful efforts, of Mrs. F[ai]r & Miss L[ooku]p and somehow of other get hold of Miss Lindsay's arm—my heart thawed into melting pleasure after being so long frozen up in the Greenland bay of Indifference amid the noise and nonsense of Edinr.—Miss seems very well pleased with my Bardship's distinguishing her, and after some slight qualms which I could easily mark, she sets the titter round at defiance, and kindly allows me to keep my hold; and when parted by the ceremony of my introduction to Mr Somerville she met me half to resume my [hold–*deleted*] situation—Nota Bene—The Poet within a point and a half of being damnably in love—I am afraid my bosom still nearly as much tinder as ever—

The old, cross-grained, whiggish, ugly, slanderous hag, Miss Lookup with all the poisonous spleen of a disappointed, ancient maid, stops me very unseasonably to [fall abusively foul–*deleted*] ease her hell-rankling bursting breast by falling [foul–*deleted*] abusively foul on the Miss Lindsays, particularly my Dulcinea; I hardly refrain from cursing her to her face— May she, for her pains, be curst with eternal desire and damn'd with endless disappointment! Hear me, O Heavens, and give ear, O Earth! may the burden of antiquated Virginity crush her down to the lowest regions of the bottomless Pit! for daring to mouth her calumnious slander on one of the finest pieces of the workmanship of Almighty Excellence. Sup at Mr. F[air's] vexed that the Miss Lindsays are not of the supper party as they only are wanting—Mrs. F[air] & Miss L[ooku]p still improve infernally on my hands—

Set out next morning [*10 May*] for Wauchope the seat of my correspondent Mrs. Scot[36]—breakfast by the way with Dr. Elliot[37] an agreable, good-hear[ted-] climate-beaten, old veteran in the medical line; now retired to a romantic but rather moorish place on the banks of the Roole[38]—he accompanies us almost to Wauchope—we traverse the country to the top of Bonchester, the scene of an old encampment, & Woolee hill—Wauchope—Mr. Scot exactly the figure [commo–*deleted*]

and face commonly given to Sancho Pança[39]—very shrewd in
his farming matters and not unfrequently stumbles on what
may be called a strong thing rather than a good thing, but in
other respects a compleat Hottentot—Mrs. S[*cott*] all the
sense, taste, intrepidity of face, & bold, critical decision which
usually distinguish female Authors—Sup with Mr Potts—[a
fine-*deleted*] agreable Partie—Breakfast next morning [*11
May*] with Mr Sommerville—the bruit of Miss Lindsay and
my Bardship by means of the invention & malice of Miss
L[*ooku*]p—Mr Sommerville sends to Dr Lindsay begging him
& family to breakfast [but at all ev-*deleted*] if convenient, but
at all events to send Miss L[*indsay*] accordingly Miss L[*indsay*]
only comes—I find Miss L[*indsay*] would soon play the devil
with me—I meet with some little flattering attentions from
her—

Mrs S[*ommerville*] an excellent, motherl[*y*], agreable woman,
and a fine famil[*y*]—Mr. Ainslie & Mr. S[*ommerville*] Junrs.
with Mr Fair, Miss Lindsay and me, go to see Esther,[40] a very
remarkable woman for reciting Poetry of all kinds, and sometimes making Scotch doggerel herself—She can repeat by
heart almost every thing she has ever read, particularly
Pope's Homer[41] from end to end—has studied Euclid by
herself, and in short is a woman of very extraordinary abilities
—on conversing with her I find her fully to come up to the
character given of her—She is very much flattered that I send
for her, and that she sees a Poet who has put out a book[42] as
she says—She is, among other things, a great Florist—and
is rather past the meridian of once celebrated beauty but
alas! tho very well married, before that period she was
violently suspected for some of the tricks of the Cytherean
Déesse[43]—

I walk down Esther's garden with Miss L[*indsay*] and after
some little chit-chat of the tender kind I presented her with a
proof-print of my nob,[44] which she accepted with something
more tender than gratitude—She told me many little stories
which Miss L[*ooku*]p had retailed concerning her and me, with
prolonging pleasure—God bless her!

Was waited on by the Magistrates and presented with the freedom of the burgh[45]—

Took farewell to Jedburgh with some melancholy, disagreable sensations—Jed, pure be thy chrystal streams, and hallowed thy sylvan banks! Sweet Isabella Lindsay, may Peace dwell in thy bosom, uninterrupted, except by the tumultuous throbbings of rapturous Love! That love-kindling eye must beam on another, not me; that graceful form must bless another's arms, not mine!

Kelso—dine with the farmer's club—all gentlemen, talking of high matters—each of them keeps a hunter from 30 to 50 £ value, and attend the fox-huntings in the country—go out with Mr Ker.[46] one of the club, [to lie–*deleted*] and a friend of Mr. Ainslie's, to lie—Mr Ker a most gentleman[*l*]y, clever, handsome fellow, a widower with some fine children—his mind & manner astonishingly like my dear old friend Robert Muir[47] in Kilmarnock—every thing in Mr. Ker's most elegant —he offers to accompany me in my English tour—dine next day [*12 May*], a devilish wet day, with Sir Alexr. Don—Sir A[*lexander*] D[*on*] a pretty clever fellow but little in him— far, far from being a match for his divine lady[48]—poverty & pride the reigning features of the family—lie at Stodrig[49] again; and set out [*Sunday, 13 May*] for Melrose—Visit Dryburgh, a fine old ruined Abbey,[50] by the way—Still bad weather—cross Leader[*river*] & come up Tweed to Melrose[51]— dine there and visit that far-fam'd glorious ruins—Come to Selkirk,[52] up Ettrick the whole country [on T–*deleted*] hereabout, both on Tweed and Ettrick, remarkably stony— [*Burns did not visit the Vale of Yarrow*].[53]

Monday [*14 May*]

Come to Inverleithing[54] a famous Spaw, & in the vicinity of the palace of Traquair,[55] where having dined, and drank some Galloway-whey, I here remain till tomorrow—saw Elibanks & Elibraes so famous in baudy song today—on the other side of Tweed—[56]

Tuesday [*15 May*]

drank tea yesternight at Pirn with Mr Horseburgh.[57]

Breakfasted today with Mr Ballantine of Hollowlee—
Proposal for a four-horse team to consist of Mr. Scot of
Wauchope Fittie-land; Logan of Logan Fittie-furr; Ballantine
of Hollowlee Forewynd; Hor[se] burgh of Horseburgh
Forefurr—Dine at a country Inn, kept by a Miller, in
Earlston,[58] the birth-place and residence of the celebrated
Thomas A Rhymer[59]—saw the ruins of his castle[60]—Come to
Berrywell—

Wedensday [*16 May*]—dined at Dunse with the farmer's
club—Company—impossible to do them justice—Revd. Mr
Smith[61] a famous Punster and Mr Meikle[62] a celebrated
Mechanic and inventor of the threshing-mills—lie again
at Berrywell—

Thursday [*17 May*] breakfast at Berrywell[63] & walk into
Dunse—To see a famous knife made by a Cutler[64] in Dunse and
to be presented to an Italian Prince[65]—A pleasant ride with
my friend Mr Robt Ainslie & his angelic sister to Mr Thomson's
a man who has newly commenced farmer, & has married a
Miss Patty Grieve formerly a flame of Mr R. Ainslie's—
company—Miss Jacky Grieve an amiable sister of Mrs Thomson's and Mr Hood[66] an honest, worthy facetious farmer in
the neighbourhood[67]—

Friday [*18 May*]—ride to Berwick[68] [*probably via Manderston,
Chirnside, Foulden, Edrington, Mordington, and Halidon
Hill*[69]]—An idle town, but rudely picturesque—Meet Lord
Errol[70] in walking round the walls—his Lordship's flattering
notice of me—dine with Mr Clunzie[71] Mercht—nothing
particular in company or conversation—come up a bold shore
& over a wild country [*ie, via Burnmouth*] to Eyemouth[72]—sup
& sleep at Mr Grieve's—

Saturday [*19 May*]—spend the day at Mr Grieve's[73]—Made a
royal arch Mason of St. Ebbe's Lodge[74]—Mr Wm Grieve, the
eldest brother, a joyous, warm-hearted, jolly, clever fellow—
takes a hearty glass & sings a good song—Mr Robt [*Grieve*] his
brother and partner in trade a good fellow but says little—Mr
[*name left blank*][75] Schoolmaster, of the partie an agreeable

1 Robert Burns in travelling clothes, by Alexander Nasmyth.

2   Robert Ainslie (1766–1838).

3　The Tweed at Coldstream Bridge (*Author's collection*).

4　Floors Castle, Roxburghshire.

5   Kelso Abbey, Roxburghshire.

6 The ruins of Roxburgh Castle from the River Tweed.

7 Jedburgh Abbey, Roxburghshire, 1790.

8   Rev. Dr Thomas Somerville
(1741–1830), Minister at
Jedburgh.

9   Wauchope House, Roxburghshire.

10 Robert Burns in the year
of his Border tour,
by Alexander Nasmyth.

11 The John Beugo
engraving of
Robert Burns.

12   The Cross, Melrose, Roxburghshire.

13   Melrose Abbey in 1790.

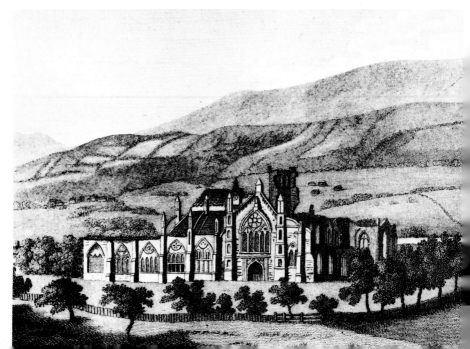

14 Dryburgh Abbey, Berwickshire in 1790.

15 Traquair House, Peeblesshire.

16   Elibank, Selkirkshire.

17   Pirn House, Peeblesshire.

18   Andrew Meikle
     (1719–1811).

19   Old Wells House.

20 Berwick-upon-Tweed from Tweedmouth foreshore.

21 Eighteenth-century view of Coldingham Priory, Berwickshire.

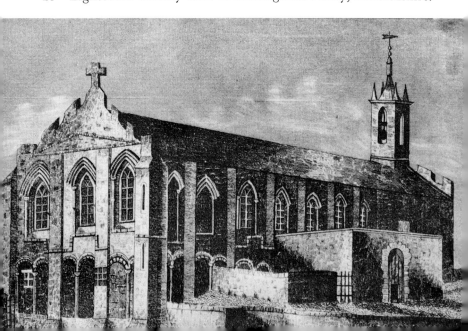

22 Robert Burns in Masonic Regalia of the St James Tarbolton
Kilwinning Lodge.

23 Pease Dene and Bridge, Berwickshire.

24 Provost Fall's House (centre portion of the building), Dunbar.

25 Sir James Hall
of Dunglass
(1761–1832).

26 Archibald Swinton
of Kimmerghame
by Joshua Reynolds.

27 **Kimmerghame House, Berwickshire, 1819** (*Author's collection*).

28 **Market Place, Alnwick, Northumberland.**

29　Alnwick Castle, *c.* 1787.

30　Warkworth Castle, Northumberland.

31   Morpeth, Northumberland.

32   Newcastle just prior to Burns's visit.

33   Hexham, Northumberland.

34   Carlisle.

35   The Malt Shovel Inn, Carlisle.

36   Carlisle Town Hall, where Burns was fined.

fellow—take a sail after dinner—fishing of all kinds pays
tithes at Eyemouth—
Sunday [*20 May*]—A Mr Robinson, a Brewer at Ednam sets
out with us for Dunbar—
The Miss Grieves very good girls—My Bardship's heart got
a brush from Miss Betsy—
Mr Willm Grieve's attachment to the family-circle so fond
that when he is out, which by the by is often the case, he
cannot go to bed till he see if all his sisters are sleeping well—
pass the famous Abbey of Coldingham[76] & Pease bridge—call
at Mr Sheriff's[77] where Mr. A[*inslie*] & I dine—Mr. S[*herriff*] a
talkative, conceited Idiot—I talk of love to Nancy [*Sherriff*]
all the evening while her brother escorts home some companions like himself—Sir James Hall of Dunglass[78] having
heard of my being in the neighbourhood comes to Mr Sher[*r*]iff's
to breakfast—takes me to see his fine scenery on the stream of
Dunglass—Dunglas[*s*] the most romantic sweet place I ever
saw—Sir James & his lady a pleasant happy couple—Sir
James shows me a favourite spot beneath an oak where Lady
Helen used to ponder on her lover Sir James being then
abroad—he points out likewise a walk for which he has an
uncommon respect as it was made by an Aunt of his to whom
he owed much—Miss [*Nancy Sherriff*] will accompany me to
Dunbar [*Robert Ainslie had by this time it appears parted company with Burns, to return to Edinburgh*] by way of making a
parade of me as a sweetheart of her among her relations—she
mounts an old cart horse as huge and as lean as a house, a
rusty old side saddle without girth or stirrup but fastened on
with an old pillion girth—herself as fine as hands could make
her in cream colored riding clothes, hat & feather, &c. I,
ashamed of my situation, ride like the devil and almost shake
her to pieces on old Jolly [*ie, the horse*]—get rid of her by refus-
ing to call at her uncle's—with her—
Past thro' the most glorious corn country [*via Cockburns-
path, Innerwick, Barns Ness*] I ever saw till I reach Dunbar[79] a
neat little town—dine with Provost Fall[80] an eminent Mercht.
and most respectable character but undescribable as he

[has no–*deleted*] exhibits no marked traits—Mrs. Fall a genius in painting, fully more clever in the fine arts & sciences then [*sic*] my friend Lady Wauchope[81] without her consummate assurance of her own abilities—Call with Mr Robinson (who, by the by, I find to be a worthy much respected man, very modest, warm, social heart which with less good sense than his would be perhaps with the children of prim precision & pride rather inimacal to that respect which is man's due from man) with him I call on Miss Clarke,[82] a maiden, in the Scotch phrase, 'Guid enough but no brent new,' a clever woman, with tolerable pretensions to remark and wit; while Time had blown the blushing bud of bashful modesty into the full-bosomed flower of easy confidence—She wanted to see what sort of raree show an Author was; and to let him know that though Dunbar was but a little town yet it was not destitute of people of parts.—

Breakfast next morning [*22 May*] at Skateraw,[83] a Mr Lee's,[84] a farmer of great note—Mr Lee an excellent, hospitable, social fellow, rather oldish, warm-hearted & chatty—a most judicious sensible farmer—Mr Lee detains me till next [day–*deleted*] morning [*23 May*]—comp. at dinner—my revd acquaintance Dr Bowmaker, a revd., rattling, drunken old fellow—two sea Lieutenants; a Mr D. Lee, a cousin of the Landlord's, a fellow whose looks are of that kind which deceived me in a gentleman at Kelso, and has often deceived me; a goodly, handsome figure and face which incline one to give them credit for parts which they have not—Mr Clarke,[85] a much cleverer fellow, but whose looks a little cloudy and his appearance rather ungainly, [make rather–*deleted*] with an every-day Observer may prejudice the opinion against him—Dr. Brown,[86] a medical young Gent. from Dunbar, a fellow whose face & manner are open and engaging—Leaving Skateraw for Dunse next day along with Collector Lorimer,[87] a lad of slender abilities and bashfully diffident to an extreme—

Found Miss Ainslie, the amiable, the sensible, the good-humored, the sweet Miss Ainslie all alone at Berrywell—Heavenly Powers who know the weaknesses of human hearts support mine! what happiness must I see only to remind me that I cannot enjoy it!

Lammermuir hills from East Lothian to Dunse, very wild—Dine with the Farmer's club at Kelso.—Sir J[oh]n Hume[88] & Mr Lumsden[89] there but nothing worth remembering when the following circumstance is considered—I walk in to Dunse before dinner, & out to Berrywell in the evening with Miss Ainslie—how well-bred, how frank, how good she is! I could grasp her with rapture on a bed of straw, and rise with contentment to the most sweltering drudgery of stiffening Labor!

[Thursday–*deleted*]—Mr. Kerr & I set out for to dine at Mr Hood's on our way to England—

Charming Rachel! [*Ainslie*] may thy bosom never be wrung by the evils of this life of sorrows, or by the villainy of this world's sons!

I am taken extremely ill with strong feverish symptoms, & take a servant of Mr Hood's to watch me all night[90]—embittering Remorse scares my fancy at the gloomy forebodings of death—I am determined to live for the future in such a manner as not to be scared at the approach of Death—I am sure I could meet him with indifference, but for 'The Something beyond the grave'—Mr. Hood agrees to accompany us to England if we will wait him till Sunday—

[Thursday–*deleted*]

Friday [*25 May*]

I go with Mr Hood to see the roup [*ie, auction sale*] of an unfortunate Farmer's stock—rigid Economy & decent Industry, do you preserve me from being the principal Dramatis Persona in such a scene of horrors! Meet my good old friend Mr. Ainslie who calls on mr Hood in the evening to take farewell of my Bardship—this day I feel myself warm wt. sentiments of gratitude to the Great Preserver of men who has kindly restored me to health and strength once more—A pleasant walk with my young friend Douglas Ainslie, a sweet, modest, clever young fellow—

Saturday [*26 May*]

ride out with Mr Hood to see the curiosities at Mr Swinton's,[91] his Landlord—fine collection of Persian & other Oriental paintings, Boydell's Prints,[92] &c.—

Sunday—27th May

Cross Tweed an[*d*] traverse the moors [*via Wooler*] thro' a wild country till I reach Alnwick[93]—Alnwick castle, a seat of the Duke of Northumberland, furnished in a most princely manner—A Mr Wilkin,[94] an Agent of His grace's, shows us the house & policies—Mr W[*ilkin*] a discreet, sensible, ingenious man—

Monday [*28 May*]

Come, still through byways, [*to*] Warworth[95] [*sic*] where we dine—hermitage & old castle—Warkworth situated very picturesque with Coquet-Island, a small rocky spot the seat of an old monastery, facing it a little in the sea; and the small but romantic river Coquet running through it—Sleep at Morpeth[96] a pleasant little town, and on next day [*29 May*] to Newcastle —Meet with a very agreable sensible fellow, a Mr. Chattox,[97] a Scotchman, who shows us a great many civilities and who dines & sups with us—

[Tuesday–*deleted*]

[*The following journal entries, printed by Allan Cunningham, are not now with the original MS.*]

Wednesday [*30 May*]—Left Newcastle[98] early in the morning and rode over a fine country to Hexham[99] to breakfast— from Hexham to Wardrue,[100] the celebrated Spa, where we slept.

Thursday [*31 May*]—Reach Longtown[101] to dine, and part there with my good friends Messrs Hood and Ker.—A hiring day in Longtown.—I am uncommonly happy to see so many young folks enjoying life.—I come to Carlisle.[102] (Meet a strange enough romantic adventure by the way, in falling in with a girl and her married sister—the girl, after some overtures of gallantry on my side, sees me a little cut with the bottle, and offers to take me in for a Gretna-green affair [*ie, an elopement*]. I, not being quite such a gull as she imagines, make an appointment with her, by way of vive la bagatelle, to hold a conference on it when we reach town.—I meet her in town and give her a brush of caressing and a bottle of cyder; but finding herself un peu trompée in her man, she sheers off.) Next day [*1 June*] I meet my good friend, Mr Mitchell,[103] and walk with him round the town and its environs, and through his printing-works, &c.—four or five hundred people employed, many of them women and children.—Dine with Mr Mitchell, and leave Carlisle.—Come by the coast to Annan.[104]—Overtaken on the way by a curious old fish of a shoemaker, and miner from Cumberland mines.

[*From Annan, Burns journeyed to Dumfries and thence through Sanquhar, to Mauchline in Ayrshire; he arrived 8 June 1787.*]

['*Here,*' *noted Allan Cunningham,* '*the Manuscript abruptly ends.*' *It contains, however, the following miscellaneous notes:*]

Kilmarnock 15th [*probably June*] 1787. Recd. from Mr Robt. Muir[105] eleven pounds ten shillings Sterl. to acct of copies of my book sent to him.—

Do from Do on same acct one pound five shillings
Do from Do on same acct two pounds ten shillings

To Miss F[*errier*][106]
[*Nae heathen I here—deleted*]
Nae heathen name shall I prefix
O' gentry frae Parnassus;
*Auld Reekie dings them a' to sticks**
For rhyme-inspiring lasses—

Tune, Duncan Davison
There was a lass they ca'd her Meg[107]
The brawest lass in a' the town
And mony a lad her love did beg
Thro' a' the country round and round

---

* [Edinburgh beats them all].

[*Here follows what is apparently the first draft of the elegy* On the Death of Sir James Hunter Blair. *The greater part of the first and second stanzas, and the whole of the tenth, are written in ink; the remainder, in pencil, is almost completely illegible.*][108]

Glasgow 1st. April 1778 G. Arms. Spiers, Mur, & Co. Mo 17/107
Do Thistle bank 12/294 2d Aug: 1783
these two five £ notes sent by post to my brother

[*A page of illegible pencilled memoranda follows*]

James Hog, Shoemaker, Buchanan's Land, head of the Cannongate—
Miss Russell No 20 Great Mary le bon, London
Mem. To enquire for a Mr Clarke,[109] Rector of a grammar School somewhere about Saltcoats or Irvine
Direct for Dr Moore[110] To Major Moore M.P. Clifford Street, Burlington Gardens—
Jas. Candlish[111]—at Mrs Barrs first land above the Crosswell Glasgow [*Not in Burns's hand*]

> *We'll aiblins get a flyte and aiblins nane*
> *We'll say it was fan ye fell o'er the stane*
> *And hurt sae sair as coudna rise your lane!*[112]

Memorandum—to write out the preceeding part of this Poem for Mrs Fall—Dunbar.
Whitelaw 3 miles from Haddington 7 miles from Dunbar 250 pr, Annum
Willm Lumsden, W.S. Apply to
19 miles from Edr. 1 mile from Leably Sinclair[113]
Edinr August 14th 1787
Payed to Mr Miers[114] for two profiles on account of Mr Aiken, Ayr, 15 sh.—
Whope, a glen between two hills—
Parreck, to force a ewe to Mother an alien lamb by closing them up together—

Notes

1. *Merse:* the name variously applied to include the whole of Berwickshire, or the southern part of the county only, or that part lying between the Lammermuirs and the Tweed, including the part of Roxburghshire north of the Tweed. As an old political term, it designated all the country between the Lammermuirs and the Cheviots, and was called a March from its position between England and Scotland; the title Earl of March was long held by the Earl of Wemyss. It is the largest and richest tract of agricultural land in Scotland.

2. *Berrywell:* the house still stands and is located on the Duns–Sinclairshill road about half a mile from where this road meets the main Berwick–Duns highway.

3. *Robert Ainslie Sr:* father of Burns's travelling companion. Ainslie the elder presented Burns, when he was leaving, with a copy of the *Letters of Junius,* 'in testimony of the most sincere friendship and esteem'.

4. *Mrs Robert Ainslie Sr:* Robert Ainslie's mother.

5. *Miss Rachel Ainslie* (b. 1768): Robert Ainslie's sister. Writing to Robert Ainslie from Mauchline on 23 July 1787, Burns asked after, 'my friend Rachel, who is far before Rachel of old, as she was before her blear-eyed sister Leah'.

6. *Douglas Ainslie* (1771–1850): Robert Ainslie's brother. He succeeded his father as lawyer and land steward to Lord Douglas's estates in Berwickshire, and made a considerable fortune. He later bought Cairnbank in Berwickshire, but died at Eden Bank, near Banff. In a letter of 23 July 1787 to Robert Ainslie, Burns asked after 'that strapping chield [*fellow*] your brother Douglas'.

7. *African:* It was rather uncommon for a Border laird to have a negro servant.

8. *William Dudgeon* (*c.* 1753–1813): A Berwickshire poet of local reputation, whose song 'Up among yon cliffy rocks', enjoyed a great deal of contemporary local popularity. Born at Tyningham, E. Lothian, Dudgeon was a farmer all his life and died at Newmains, Whitekirk.

[29]

9. *Dunse:* now Duns, the spelling was officially altered in 1882. Founded in 1583, the town takes its name from the nearby hill, Duns Law. The county town of Berwickshire.

10. *Rev. Dr. Robert Bowmaker* (1731–97): ordained to the parish of Duns in 1769. His church was the original parish church of Duns, just off Market Square and is not to be confused with the South Church which is quite near it. Tradition has it that Duns parish church, as an institution, dates back to Norman times. Undoubtedly, it was repaired in 1572, but the church Burns knew was wholly demolished in 1790. A new church was erected in 1792, but was destroyed by fire in 1879; it was restored once more in 1880 in the form of the present building.

11. While at church Burns noticed Rachel Ainslie hunting for the text of Bowmaker's sermon, which was on obstinate sinners. Burns scribbled the following impromptu lines and passed them to her:

> *Fair maid, you need not take the hint,*
> *Nor idle texts pursue:*
> *'Twas guilty sinners that he meant*
> *Not Angels such as you!*

12. *Coldstream:* once called Lennel, a burgh on the Tweed, Berwickshire. Once a refuge for eloping couples, the Coldstream guards were raised near here in 1659.

13. *Cornhill:* a small village in N. Northumberland, once famous for its medicinal wells.

14. Smeaton's five-arched bridge (1763–6). Long afterwards Robert Ainslie told Poet James Hogg (in a letter dated 20 April 1834) how Burns on stepping onto English soil doffed his blue bonnet, and kneeling on the turf by the roadside, prayed and invoked a blessing on Scotland in the words of the closing two stanzas of his 'Cotter's Saturday Night':

> *O Scotia! my dear, my native soil!*
> *For whom my warmest wish to heaven is sent!*
> *Long may thy hardy sons of rustic toil,*
> *Be blest with health, and peace, and sweet content!*
> *And O may Heaven their simple lives prevent*
> *From Luxury's contagion, weak and vile!*
> *Then howe'er crowns and coronets be rent,*
> *A virtuous Populace may rise the while,*
> *And stand a wall of fire, around their much-lov'd Isle.*

O Thou! who pour'd the patriotic tide,
   That stream'd thro' great, unhappy Wallace' heart;
Who dar'd to, nobly, stem tyrannic pride,
   Or nobly die, the second glorious part:
(The Patriot's GOD, peculiarly thou art,
   His friend, inspirer, guardian and reward!)
O never, never Scotia's realm desert,
   But still the Patriot, and the Patriot-Bard,
In bright succession raise, her Ornament and Guard!

Most probably this story is apocryphal, and no more than a piece of parochial tusherie.

15. *Foreman:* a local farmer.

16. *François-Marie Arouet de Voltaire* (1694–1778): one of the greatest French philosophers and writers.

17. *Patrick Brydone* (1736–1818): traveller and author, son of Robert Brydone, parish minister of Coldingham. His *A Tour of Sicily and Malta* (1773) went through many editions. He accompanied Col. William Fullarton (1754–1808), whom Burns later met in 1791, on his tour of Europe. Brydone's wife was a daughter of Robertson the historian. The present Lennel house was built after 1787.

18. *Kelso:* A border town on the river Tweed, 42 miles south of Edinburgh; at the meeting of the Tweed and the Teviot. Sir Walter Scott had been a pupil at the old grammar school in 1783.

19. The bridge which took Burns's fancy was washed away by the great flood of 26 October 1797. It was replaced by Rennie's five-arched bridge between 1800–3. See plate 3.

20. *Mr Scot:* Robert Scott was appointed Kelso agent for the Bank of Scotland in 1774; he had been formerly employed as Agent to the Duke of Buccleuch.

21. *Roxburgh Palace:* Burns was referring to Floors Castle, the seat of the Duke of Roxburghe, one mile west of Kelso. See plate 4.

22. The ruins of the Tironesian Abbey, founded in 1128 by David I. See plate 5.

23. *Caverton:* A hamlet in north-east Roxburghshire. David McDowal's family had been farmers in the district of Kaewater since the late 1500s.

24. *Jedburgh:* A border town on the river Jed. Mary Queen of Scots lodged here when she came to open the Justice Aire, or Circuit Court, in October 1566. Prince Charles Edward Stuart stayed in the Castlegate for a night in 1745. The English poet William Wordsworth lodged at 5 Abbey Close in 1803. Burns lodged at

27 Canongate adjoining Dean's Close (plaque erected 1913). At that time Burns' lodging would be one of the chief houses in the burgh: 'The rooms [*were*] large, and the marble jambs and carved woodwork round the fireplace of the largest room are relics of [*sixteenth century*] grandeur.'

25. *James Fair* (d. 1796): Lawyer, whose sight had been impaired by the ineptitude of a quack. He purchased the estate of Langlee and married Catherine Lookup. For a time Fair was Agent for the British Linen Bank.

26. *Writer:* ie, to His Majesty's Signet—a lawyer.

27. *roup of parks:* a land auction.

28. *John Rutherford* (1746–1830): Sent to New York under the care of his uncle Walter in 1761, during an expedition to the Canadian outback out of Fort Detroit, Rutherford was captured by Chippewah Indians, and was held by them for some time as a slave. On his rescue, Rutherford pursued a military career in the 42nd Regiment based at New York. After he retired he acquired the estate of Mossburnford, and it was here where Burns visited him.

29. *Jedburgh Abbey:* Founded in 1128 by David I for Augustinian canons regular. This abbey possesses the only complete, or nearly complete, Transitional west front in Scotland. See plate 7.

30. *Mr Potts:* A check of the History of the Faculty of Advocates at Edinburgh shows that no-one of this name was registered as a Writer to the Signet in 1787. Potts may have been an English lawyer.

31. *The Reverend Dr Thomas Somerville* (1741–1830): Minister at Jedburgh and author of a *History of Great Britain during the Reign of Queen Anne* (1798) (see plate 8). His niece and daughter-in-law was the mathematician and physicist Mrs Mary Somerville. Local legend has it that Somerville gave up the punning habit when he read this extract in Currie's memoir of Burns. Somerville's most important book *My Own Life and Times,* is a valuable and interesting journal chronicling local and national affairs 1741–1814.

32. *half-ell:* a common dialect pun for a large mouth—an ell was a cloth measure of 1¼ yards.

33. *Miss Hope:* One of the Hopes of Cowdenknowes.

34. *Isabella Lindsay* (b. 1764): Daughter of the Jedburgh doctor Robert Lindsay. She married Adam Armstrong twenty-four days after parting with Burns: In view of her engagement, she was apparently much criticised locally for her 'easy manners' with Burns, with whom she obviously had a mild flirtation. As her husband was in the employ of the Russian Government, Isabella went with him, never to return to Scotland. At the time of Burns's

visit, Dr Lindsay occupied the house which had been associated with Mary Queen of Scots. Miss Lindsay's sister, Peggy, herein mentioned, died not long after Burns's visit at the age of 22.

35. *bonie*—pretty; *strappan*—tall, handsome; *sonsie*—comely.

36. *Mrs Elizabeth Scott, nee Rutherford* (1729–89): Mrs Scott, wife of Walter Scott of Wauchope House, nr Jedburgh, had sent Burns a long verse epistle, offering him a marled plaid [*ie, a mottled shoulder blanket*] in token of her admiration of his work: Burns had replied with his own lively verse epistle, *The Answer to the Gudewife of Wauchope House* (March 1787). A niece of Mrs Alison Cockburn (1712–94), of 'The Flowers of the Forest' fame, Mrs Scott's poems were published in 1801 under the title of *Alonza and Cora,* in which her address to Burns was featured. (See Appendix II).

37. *Gilbert Elliot* (b. 1717): Surgeon to his cousin General George Augustus Elliot's regiment of light horse, which was to be known as the 15th Hussars. While breakfasting with this Elliot of Otterburn at Wells on Rule (Plate 19), Burns (it is said) much admired a chair which had been the property of James Thomson (1700–48), author of 'The Seasons'. Thomson had been born at Ednam manse, Kelso, and was educated at Jedburgh.

38. Now known as the Rule Water, which joins the Teviot.

39. *Sancho Panza:* Esquire to Don Quixote in *Don Quixote of La Mancha* (1695, 1615) by Miguel de Cervantes. This is Burns's second allusion to Cervantes's classic—see above 'Dulcinea', a reference to Quixote's sweetheart.

40. *Esther Easton:* Lived in a house on the Lindsay property. The wife of a poor gardener, she kept school for a short while. Died 1789.

41. *Alexander Pope* (1688–1744); *Translations of Homer* (1715–26).

42. By this time, of course, two editions of Burns's poems had been published: Kilmarnock Edition, 31 July 1786; First Edinburgh Edition, 21 April 1787.

43. Burns means here that Esther was considered wanton, Cytherean being a common eighteenth-century euphemism for a prostitute.

44. Burns was probably referring to the stipple engraving so recently done for him by John Beugo (1759–1841) the famed Edinburgh engraver. Writing to John Ballantine (1743–1812), the merchant and banker of Ayr—and his early patron—on 24 February 1787 Burns noted: 'I am getting my phiz done, by an eminent engraver, and if it be ready in time, I will appear in my book [*First Edinburgh Edition*], looking like all other *fools* to my title-page.' Burns received thirty-six India proofs of this print and

distributed them among friends: surviving copies òf these prints are now very rare and to be extremely valued. See plate 11.

45. Burns, however, did not sign the Jedburgh burgess roll. Until 1939 his burgess ticket was thought lost, but in that year it was put up for sale. At the time Jedburgh was unable to raise the money to buy it back, but it was returned to Jedburgh in 1971. The ticket records that: '[*On 11 May 1787*] Robert Burns Esquire was entered and received into the Libertys of this Burgh, Create and made a free Burges and Guild Brother of the same, who gave his Oath with all Ceremonies used and wont. Whereupon He required Acts of Court and protested for an Extract of the same under the Common Seal of the Burgh.'

Robert Chambers in his 1856 edition of *The Life and Works of Robert Burns* added notes concerning Burns's being presented with the freedom of the burgh: 'On this occasion the usual treat of a *riddle of claret* was bestowed upon the bard in the inn. Always jealous of his independence, he left the room before the feast was over, and endeavoured to induce the landlord to accept of payment of the gill from *him*. It is scarcely necessary to say, that mine host knew too well what was befitting the dignity of the Burgh to take Burns's money. . . .'

46. *Mr Ker:* Robert Kerr, farmer in Roxburghshire.

47. *Robert Muir* (1758–88): A Kilmarnock wine merchant whom Burns had first met in 1786. An ailing man who died of consumption, Muir subscribed for 72 copies of the Kilmarnock Edition and 40 of the First Edinburgh Edition of Burns's poems.

48. *Lady Henrietta Don* (1752–1801): Wife of Sir Alexander Don (d. 1815) of Newton Don, Berwickshire. She was the elder daughter of the thirteenth Earl of Glencairn and sister to Earl James, Burns's patron. She was in receipt of a parcel of Burns's self-styled 'epistolary performances' which today make up the Don Manuscript, now in the Library of the University of Edinburgh. This manuscript of letters and poems was bequeathed to the Library in 1878 by David Laing, an assiduous purchaser of manuscripts; unfortunately Laing gave no indication as to how he came by the manuscripts.

49. *Stodrig:* A farm in Roxburghshire, long worked by the Usher family.

50. *Dryburgh:* Berwickshire, 3½ miles south-east of Melrose: The Abbey founded by Hugh de Morville in the reign of David I (1124–53) was a house of Premonstratensian canons. Within the present ruins are the graves of Sir Walter Scott and Earl Haig.

51. *Melrose:* Market town of Roxburghshire. The Cistercian Abbey here was founded by David I. Somewhere in the church is

said to lie buried the heart of King Robert the Bruce. See plates 12 & 13.

52. *Selkirk:* Royal and muncipal burgh dating from 1113. Sir Walter Scott served here as sheriff of the county. In his *Life of Robert Burns* (1888), John Stuart Blackie recounts the Selkirk incident which he attributes to James Hogg:

> I have often heard Dr Clarkson tell . . . that when Mr Ainslie and Burns arrived in Selkirk that evening, they were just like 'twa drookit craws'. The doctor and other two gentlemen were sitting in Veitch's Inn, near the West Port, taking their glass . . . When the travellers arrived, the trio within viewed them from the window as they alighted, and certainly conceived no very high opinion of them. In a short time, however, they sent Mr Veitch to the doctor and his friends, requesting permission for two strangers to take a glass with them. The doctor objected, and asked Mr Veitch what the men were like. Mr Veitch said he could not well say; the one spoke rather like a gentleman, but the other was a drover-looking chap; so they refused to admit them, sending them word that they were sorry they were engaged elsewhere, and obliged to go away. The doctor saw them riding off next morning; and it was not till the third day, that he learned it had been the celebrated Scotch poet whom they had refused to admit. That refusal hangs about the doctor's heart like a dead-weight to this day, and will do till the day of his death, for the bard had not a more enthusiastic admirer.

Today a plaque marks the site of the old Forest Inn, Selkirk. While at Selkirk Burns wrote to his publisher William Creech (See Appendix I).

53. It is strange that Burns did not visit the famous Vale of Yarrow. Undoubtedly one of the most beautiful of Border scenes, Yarrow gives its name to a river and a parish in Selkirkshire, and has been much lauded by balladists, for example in the tragedy *The Dowie Dens of Yarrow.*

54. *Inverleithing:* Innerleithen, Peeblesshire. The earliest mention of Innerleithen is in the reign of Malcolm IV in the twelfth century, when the parish church was given by the monarch to the monks of Kelso. When Burns visited the village it was a collection of thatched cottages irregularly spaced out. Burns stayed at the inn then to be found in Piccadilly (now the High Street): This thatched inn was demolished in the 1860s, but a plaque was erected on the site in 1913.

55. *Traquair:* Traquair house, Peebleshire, once the seat of a prominent Jacobite family. See plate 15.

56. *Elibanks:* Famous as the seat of Lord Elibank, 5 miles east of Innerleithen. See Appendix III, for the reference to the 'Bawdy song', and plate 16.

57. *Horseburgh of Pirn:* On the Gala Water. Horsburghs of that Ilk, an ancient house as any in the county, have been extinct in the male line since 1911. Pirn house has been demolished. See plate 17. Burns immortalised Gala Water in his famous poem *Braw Lads o' Gala Water* written in 1792-3, and published in *Selected Scottish Airs,* I, i 1793. The theme was of course, taken from an old song.

> *Braw braw lads on Yarrow braes,*
> *They rove amang the blooming heather;*
> *But Yarrow braes¹ not Ettrick shaws*
> *Can match the lads o'Gala Water.*
>
> *But there is ane, a secret ane,*
> *Aboon them a'I lo'e him better;*
> *And I'll be his, and he'll be mine,*
> *The bonnie lad o'Gala Water.*
> *Altho' his daddie was nae laird,*
> *And tho' I hae nae meikle tocher,²*
> *Yet rich in kindest, truest love,*
> *We'll tent³ our flocks by Gala Water.*
>
> *It ne'er was wealth, it ne'er was wealth,*
> *That coft⁴ contentment, peace or pleasure;*
> *The bands and bliss o' mutual love,*
> *O that's the chiefest warld's treasure!*

58. *Earlston:* parish and village 8 miles southeast of Duns, Berwickshire. Burns probably detoured by Earlston so that he could see Cowdenknowes on the Leader Water. There is a local legend that Burns paused at nearby Greenlaw for a meal: apparently he was none too pleased with either his host or the meal set before him, which gave rise to this oft-repeated doggerel, still attributed to Burns's pen. The verse does not appear in any of the collected editions of Burns's poems:

---

¹ *copses*
² *much dowry*
³ *tend*
⁴ *purchased*

If ever I pass by this door
I'll eat that devil's head, by God!
Ane and saxpence for a dinner,
Aye, the damned confounded sinner!

59. *Thomas the Rhymer* (*c.* 1220–97): Of Erceldoune (Earlston). A great number of prophetic sayings were attributed to him, from which he got the name of 'True Thomas'. A semi-legendary figure, like Merlin, he was supposed to have been carried off to Elfland by the fairies but allowed to revisit the earth for a time. Sir Walter Scott believed him to be the author of the poem *Sir Tristrem,* which had been based on a French original. Burns probably first came across Thomas through William Hamilton's English rendition of Blind Harry the Minstrel's (d. 1492) 12,000-line poem *Wallace,* for in this the Rhymer is introduced at the Abbey of Fail (in Burns's own parish of Tarbolton) prophesying victory for the hero.

60. Burns is referring to the Rhymer's Tower, which is still to be seen.

61. *The Reverend Andrew Smith* (1741–89): Minister of Langton, in the Presbytery of Duns, from 1766–89. He married Ann Drummond, heiress to Concraig, to which estate he ultimately succeeded, and took the name of Drummond.

62. *Andrew Meikle* (1719–1811): A millwright at Houston Mill, near Dunbar. He invented the Threshing Mill in 1784, and patented it in 1788. See plate 19.

63. While at Berrywell during 17 May to 24 May Burns wrote three letters (See Appendix I).

64. Although the Burgh Records show that several metalworkers pursued their craft at Duns at the time of Burns's visit, none are identified as cutlers. Neither do the records of the Worshipful Company of Cutlers of the City of London, or those of the Edinburgh Guild of Hammermen give any listing of craft members extant in Duns at this time.

65. Scottish cutlers' work was very fashionable in Italy in the second half of the eighteenth century, but no trace has been found of an Italian prince who placed orders around this date. It is possible that the author of the famous *Lettere sopra l'Inghilterra,* Luigi Angiolini, who was in Scotland at the time, may have been the contact here.

66. *Mr Hood:* Thomas Hood, Berwickshire farmer.

67. During his stay at Berrywell Burns received several unsolicited packets of poems from a Simon Gray, who deemed himself a poet. In the accompanying letters to the poems Gray invited

Burns to comment on the verses, with a belaboured hint to be flattering. Burns penned a reply imitating Gray's own style:

To Symon Gray

I

SYMON Gray,
You're dull to-day.

II

Dulness, with redoubted sway,
Has seized the wits of Symon Gray.

III

Dear Cimon Gray,
The other day,
When you sent me some rhyme,
I could not then just ascertain
Its worth, for want of time.

But now today, good Mr. Gray,
I've read it o'er and o'er,
Tried all my skill, but find I'm still
Just where I was before.

We auld wives' minions gie our opinions,
Solicited or no;
Then of its fau'ts my honest thoughts
I'll give—and here they go.
Such damn'd bombast no time that's past
Will show, or time to come,
So, Cimon dear, your song I'll tear,
And with it wipe my [bum].

68. *Berwick:* One of the first four royal burghs of Scotland, and from 1173 to 1460 changed hands, between the Scots and English, fourteen times. In 1551 Berwick was declared neutral territory. In Burns's day Berwick's chief public building was the town hall. See plate 20.

There is a tradition, which is not really evident from the journal, that Burns took a dislike to Berwick and its burghers. According to J. Hardy in *The Denham Tracts* (The Folklore Society, 1892) many believed that Burns composed a piece of doggerel to immortalise this dislike:

> *Berwick is a dirty place.*
> *Has a church without a steeple,*
> *A middenstead at every door*
> *And a damned deceitful people.*

Hardy noted that Burns was supposed to have scratched the poem on a pane of glass in the window of his lodgings. As the doggerel does not appear in any collection of Burns's poems the story is deemed apocryphal. Hardy further quotes two alternative versions of the verse, which by the 1860s had become an old wives' tale:

1802 version:
> *Berwick is an ancient town*
> *A church without a steeple.*
> *A pretty girl at every door*
> *And very generous people.*

1820 version:
> *Berwick is a dirty town,*
> *A church without a steeple.*
> *There's a midden at every door,*
> *God curse all the people.*

69. Burns does not mention having visited John Renton of Lamerton, at Mordington House. Renton certainly sent Burns an invitation to ride and dine with him, for this note from the poet was found among Renton's papers:

> *Your billet, sir, I grant receipt;*
> *Wi' you I'll canter ony gate,*
> *Though 'twere a trip to yon blue warl',*
> *Where birkies march on burning marl:*
> *Then, sir, God willing, I'll attend ye,*
> *And to His goodness I commend ye.*

70. *George 16th Earl of Erroll* (1767–98): Representative Peer 1796. Served as Lt.-Col 1st Guards at Walcheren, Netherlands. Having inadvertently disclosed a secret entrusted to him by William Pitt, Erroll committed suicide. His mother was Isabella, daughter of Sir William Carr, Bt of Etal.

71. *John Clunie:* Freeman and Magistrate 1781. Mayor of Berwick 1783–84. A partner in Clunie and Home, Timber and Iron Merchants, Bridge St., Berwick.

72. *Eyemouth:* fishing village situated at the mouth of the river

Eye, eight miles north of the Scottish Border. In 1597 Eyemouth was made a free Burgh of Barony, with the privilege of a free port.

73. *William Grieve:* A corn merchant, who lived at Beach Villa.

74. The Masonic Lodge at Eyemouth considered it so great an honour to have such a distinguished visitor that they admitted him without charging the usual fee. The minute for 19 May 1787 records:

> At a general encampment held this day, the following brethren were made Royal Arch Masons, viz: Robert Burns from the Lodge of St. James, Tarbolton, Ayrshire, and Robert Ainslie, from the Lodge of St. Luke's Edinburgh . . . Robert Ainslie paid one guinea admission dues . . . Robert Burns . . . admit[*ted*] . . . gratis . . .

There is a Memorial Plaque to Burns on the outside wall of St Ebbe's Lodge, facing Market Place, and inside an illuminated picture of the poet. The Lodge also retains a set of bottles, cups and so on, said to have been used in Burns's repast.

Extract attested by Bro. Thomas Bowhill.

75. James Carmichael.

76. *Coldingham Priory:* founded in 1098 by Edgar of Scotland. See plate 21.

77. *Mr Sherriff:* George Sherriff, one of the Sherriffs of Long-formacus.

78. *Sir James Hall of Dunglass,* fourth Baronet (1761–1832): A chemist and geologist who wrote several papers in support of James Hutton's (1726–97) theory of the earth (1785). President of the Royal Society of Edinburgh, Sir James's son Captain Basil Hall, RN, was a friend of Sir Walter Scott. He married Lady Helen Douglas, second daughter of Dunbar, Earl of Selkirk in 1786. The present Dunglass house was built after 1787. See plate 25.

79. *Dunbar:* Burgh and fishing port of East Lothian. Famous in history for its thirteenth-century castle and Grey Friars monastery. There is a tradition that during his visit to Dunbar Burns was entertained at the Dunbar Castle Lodge No 75 of Freemasons. The records of this Lodge do not attest to any such visit; thus the story must be taken as purely apocryphal.

80. *Robert Fall* (d. 1796): Member of a wealthy merchant family. He was alleged to have been of gipsy, or 'Fa' origin. Provost Fall's house at Dunbar, once a town house of the Earl of Lauderdale, still stands, a part of a barracks, though no longer used for military purposes. See plate 24.

81. *Lady Wauchope:* Mrs Walter Scott of Wauchope. See note 36. Because she was a laird's wife she was called 'Lady'. For the use of 'Lady' to describe a laird's wife, see Sir Thomas Innes of Learney's *Tartans of the Clans and Families of Scotland,* 64–5.

82. *Miss Clarke:* A person of some local distinction, well known for her tea parties.

83. *Skateraw:* A small village 4 miles south-east of Dunbar.

84. *Mr Lee:* Farmer of Skateraw, the largest holding in the district.

85. *Mr Clarke:* Brother of the aforementioned Miss Clarke.

86. *David Brown:* Received his Licentiate's diploma at the Royal College of Surgeons, 20 March 1778.

87. *Collector Lorimer:* Charles Lorimer, who held the office of Collector of Customs at Dunbar from 22 March 1771 to 8 March 1814, when he retired on superannuation. Lorimer died in 1824.

88. *Sir John Hume* (or, Home; succ. 1737, d. 1788): of Renton in the parish of Coldingham. He had large farming interests in the Coldingham area; the baronetcy, incidentally, became apparently extinct on his death.

89. *Mr Lumsden:* A Roxburghshire farmer.

90. Probably characteristic of Burns's health record of recurrent rheumatic fever.

91. *Mr Swinton:* Archibald Swinton of Kimmergham (1731–1804), Captain in the East India Company; served under Robert Clive. See plate 26.

92. *Boydell Prints:* Those of John Boydell (1719–1804), the Shropshire born engraver and printer who became Lord Mayor of London in 1790.

93. *Alnwick:* Town some 33 miles north of Newcastle on the Aln. A very ancient market town of great historical interest. Noteworthy for the Hotspur Tower, the original gateway to the town. See plate 28.

94. *Mr Wilkin:* Thomas Wilkin (1737–98), Land Surveyor to the Dukes of Northumberland from 1771–97.

95. *Warkworth:* The earliest remains of Warkworth Castle date from the twelfth century. In the fourteenth century it came into the possession of the Percys, the Earls of Northumberland in whose family it remains. The hermitage consists of a small chapel cut in solid rock with living-rooms adjoining, which dates from the fourteenth century and is reached by boat from the castle. The hermitage is celebrated in one of Thomas Percy's ballads. See plate 30.

96. *Morpeth:* A pre-Conquest market town some sixteen miles north by west of Newcastle on the river Wansbeck. It has remains

of a twelfth century castle, Newminster (a Cistercian Abbey), and a fourteenth century parish church. See plate 31.

97. There is a local story that when Burns dined with Mr Chattox, he was startled when seeing the meat served before the soup. 'This', explained Mr Chattox jokingly, 'is in obedience to a North-umbrian maxim, which enjoins us to eat beef before we sup the broth, lest the hungry Scotch make an inroad and snatch it.'

98. While at Newcastle Burns wrote one letter. See Appendix I.

99. *Hexham:* A market town of Northumberland, situated on the south bank of the Tyne 21 miles west of Newcastle. Famous for its abbey church of St Andrew founded by Wilfred Archbishop of York in 674. The moot hall and the manor office, two castellated towers dating from the fourteenth century, would undoubtedly have caught Burns's eye. See plate 33.

100. *Wardrue:* Wardrew.

101. *Longtoun:* Market town in Cumberland on the river Esk, nine miles north-west of Carlisle. It contains the famous parish church of Arthuret.

102. *Carlisle:* County town of Cumberland, standing on a fertile tract of land nine miles from the Scottish Border, and on the rivers Eden, Caldew and Petteril. It has been an important civil and military centre since Roman times. Burns stayed at the now demolished Malt Shovel Inn, Rickergate. Here Burns wrote to William Nicol. See Appendix I and plates 34 and 35.

103. *Mr Mitchell:* Probably a partner in the firm of Mitchell, Ellwood & Co, one of the four printers operating in Carlisle in 1794. After dining with Mitchell, Burns returned to the Malt Shovel Inn to be told by the landlord Peter Reid, that his horse had been found trespassing on a piece of unenclosed corporation grass called 'the Bitts'. The horse had been impounded. In order that his horse might be released Burns had to pay a fine. He marked the occasion with an epigram lampooning the Mayor of Carlisle:

> *Was e'er puir poet sae befitted,*
> *The maister drunk—the horse committed*
> *Puir harmless beast! tak' thee nae care,*
> *Thou'lt be a horse when he's nae mair.*

In Topping's *Memories of Old Carlisle* there is mentioned a further association of Burns with Carlisle. The story goes that Burns, while out walking, lost his companions in the bustle round the market square. Knowing that they were making for a certain inn, Burns made his own way there. In an attempt to find his companions Burns searched the inn and at length put his head round the door of one room where three men were having a private drinking session: As Burns withdrew his head, one of the party called out, 'Come in, Johnny Peep'. Burns joined them and in a while was as merry as they. At length it was decided that each man should write a verse of poetry, and put it, with half-a-crown, under the candlestick, with the idea that the best poem would win back the half-a-crown while the remaining seven and sixpence would be spent on ale. Burns won the contest with:

> *Here am I, Johnny Peep,*
> *I saw three sheep,*
> *   And these three sheep saw me;*
> *Half-a-crown a-piece*
> *Will pay for their fleece,*
> *   And so Johnny Peep gets free.*

The story, however, remains apocryphal.

104. *Annan:* Royal burgh and market town on the river Annan, some fifteen miles south-east of Dumfries. Site of an ancient fortress of the Bruces. Birthplace of Hugh Clapperton the African explorer.

105. Robert Muir, one of Burns's most devoted friends. He it was who disposed of seventy-two copies of the Kilmarnock *Poems*.

106. *Jane Ferrier* (1767–1846): Eldest daughter of James Ferrier (1744–1829) the Edinburgh lawyer. A celebrated beauty and clever artist, she married General Samuel Graham, Deputy-Governor of Stirling Castle. Burns did in fact send her these lines in August 1787 which were expanded to:

> *MADAM*
> *   Nae Heathen Name shall I prefix,*
> *   Frae Pindus or Parnassus;*
> *   AULD REEKIE dings them a' to sticks*
> *   For rhyme-inspiring Lasses.—*
>
> *   Jove's tunefu' Dochters three times three*
> *   Made Homer deep their debtor;*
> *   But gien the body half an e'e,*
> *   Nine FERRIERS wad done better.—*
>
> *   Last day my mind was in a bog,*
> *   Down George's street I stoited;*
> *   A creeping, cauld PROSAIC fog*
> *   My vera senses doited.—*

Do what I dought to set her free,
  My Muse lay in the mire;
Ye turn'd a neuk—I saw your e'e—
  She took the wing like fire.—

The mournfu' Sang I here inclose,
  In GRATITUDE I send you;
And pray in rhyme, sincere as prose,
  A' GUIDE THINGS MAY ATTEND YOU.

107. Scholars cannot be certain whether these lines are Burns's own, or whether they represent a noted fragment of folkstory he subsequently re-worked. They were expanded to:

There was a lass, they ca'd her Meg,
  And she held o'er the moors to spin;
There was a lad that follow'd her,
  They ca'd him Duncan Davison.
The moor was driegh, and Meg was skiegh,
  Her favour Duncan could na win;
For wi' the rock she wad him knock,
  And ay she shook the temper-pin.

As o'er the moor they lightly foor,
  A burn, was clear a glen was green,
Upon the banks they eas'd their shanks,
  And ay she set the wheel between:
But Duncan swoor a haly aith
  That Meg should be a bride the morn,
Then Meg took up her spinnin-graith,
  And flang them a' out o'er the burn.

We will big a wee, wee house,
  And we will live like king and queen;
Sae blythe and merry's we will be,
  When ye set by the wheel at e'en.
A man may drink and no be drunk,
  A man may fight and no be slain:
A man may kiss a bony lass,
  And ay be welcome back again.

108. *Sir James Hunter Blair* (1741–87): He was born John Hunter, the son of an Ayr merchant, and became a banker with the firm of Sir William Forbes. He acquired the estate of Robertland

and married the heiress of John Blair of Dunskey in 1770. MP for Edinburgh 1780–84. He was one of Burns's kindest friends when the poet first came to Edinburgh and had 'a large company of friends' to meet the poet at breakfast at his residence 'in the eastern division of Queen Street'.

These lines are almost unique among Burns's surviving poetical manuscripts in that they are a genuine first draft. Nearly the whole of Burns's surviving manuscript poems are all fair copies of completed poems; for Burns seems to have destroyed whatever tentative jottings he began once the verses had been shaped to his satisfaction. From this pen and pencil entry it is interesting to see how far Burns's first impulse carried him in the writing of this elegy.

The following extract of the first two stanzas is written in ink:

> *The lamp of day with ill presaging glare*
> *Dim, cloudy sunk behind the western wave;*
> *Th' inconstant blast howl'd thro' the darkning air,*
>
> *Lone as I wander'd by each dell and dell,*
> *Once the lov'd haunts of Scotia's royal train;*
> *Or mused where erst revered waters*
> *Or mouldering ruins mark the sacred fane.—*

The fourth line of the first stanza was subsequently added in pencil. And in the finished version may be compared:

> *The lamp of day, with ill-presaging glare,*
> *Dim, cloudy, sunk beyond the western wave:*
> *Th'inconstant blast howl'd thro' the darkening air,*
> *And hollow whistled in the rocky cave.*
>
> *Lone as I wander'd by each cliff and dell,*
> *Once the lov'd haunts of Scotia's royal train;*
> *Or mus'd where limpid streams, once hallow'd, well;*
> *Or mouldering ruins mark the sacred Fane.*

The next six stanzas appear in the holograph with no noteworthy variants. The tenth stanza is in ink, but its second line, '*While worthless Greatness saves an empty name?*' has been altered by interlinear reversal of the adjectives to the now published form: '*While empty Greatness saves a worthless name?*' The last stanza (the eleventh) is missing.

It is interesting to note the sums of money here: For they furnish some proof of the substantial sums Burns received from his literary works: Burns, of course, was never able to save much. His brother Gilbert's bad bargain at Mossgiel cost Burns dear and his morality was an additional drain on his purse. When Burns returned to Dumfries after the Border tour he found a letter awaiting him from May Cameron, an Edinburgh servant girl, whom he had made pregnant. His reply to her was addressed to the James Hog mentioned here (and therefore was written not earlier than 2 June 1787).

109. *Mr Clarke:* Probably James Clarke (1761?–1825) who became a schoolmaster at Moffat Grammar School 1786.

110. *Dr John Moore* (1729–1802): Surgeon and topographer and novelist. Moore sent Burns copies of his *View of Society and Manners in France, Switzerland and Germany,* and his first novel *Zeluco.* The Moore–Burns relationship resulted in the famous *Autobiographical Letter* (2 Aug 1787).

111. *James Candlish* (1759–1806): A boyhood neighbour and schoolmate of Burns. He studied medicine at Glasgow University and was described by Burns in a letter to Peter Hill (March 1791) from Ellisland as: 'the earliest friend except my only brother that I have on earth, and one of the worthiest fellows that ever any man called by the name of Friend'.

112. From Alexander Ross's (1699–1784) *Helenore; or, The Fortunate Shepherdess* (lines 113–15).

113. A farm called Whitelaw is still to be found west by north of Whitelaw Hill, one of the northwesterly foothills of the Lammermuirs. Leably Sinclair is not traceable on modern maps.

114. *Mr Miers:* The skilful Edinburgh silhouettist John Miers. It is rather difficult from this to identify the 'two profiles' herein mentioned. They may have been of Burns himself, or this may only refer to pictures ordered by Robert Aiken (a lawyer from Ayr) on a visit to Edinburgh. If the profiles were of Burns, then this entry proves that the famous Miers silhouette of Burns must have been worked in the spring of 1787: To date the earliest mention of Miers in Burns's letters is in a letter to Clarinda 31 January 1788 (See Raymond Lamont Brown, *Clarinda: The Intimate Story of Robert Burns and Agnes Maclehose.* Martin Black 1968, pp 144–5 & 241–3). Burns was not in Edinburgh during 4 May—& August 1787; thus for Aiken to have seen the silhouette (and to have ordered copies), Burns must have had it with him on his return to Ayrshire.

The last lines of the entry show that Burns's assessment of Scots dialect was conscious and literary. These are strictly Border dialect words, which he jotted down, but it seems that he never had occasion to use them.

APPENDICES

I The Tour Correspondence

While on his tour of the Borders, Burns wrote seven authenticated letters. It is important to read these letters in conjunction with his journal, for they lead to a better understanding of Burns's state of mind during the tour and give some indication of the business matters which filled his thoughts as he travelled.

1 WILLIAM CREECH, Esq: London

[*Selkirk 13 May 1787*]

My honored Friend,

The inclosed I have just wrote, nearly extempore, in a solitary Inn in Selkirk, after a miserable wet day's riding—I have been over most of East Lothian, Berwick, Roxburgh & Selkirk Shires; and next week I begin a tour through the north of England.— Yesterday, I dined with Lady Hariot, sister to my noble Patron— Quem Deus conservet!—I would write till I would tire you as much with dull Prose as I dare say by this time you are with wretched Verse, but I am jaded to death; so, with a grateful farewell, I have the honor to be,

good Sir, yours sincerely ROBT BURNS

[*Printed in* Robert Hartley Cromek: *Reliques of Robert Burns; consisting chiefly of original letters, poems, and critical observations on Scottish songs* . . . London 1808.]

[*Enclosure Poem 'Willie's Awa'*]

> Auld chuckie REEKIE'S sair distrest,[1]
> Down droops her ance weel-burnish'd crest,
> Nae joy her bonie buskit[2] nest
>   Can yield ava;[3]
> Her darling bird that she lo'es best,
>   Willie's awa.—

[1] *Dear old Edinburgh is greatly distressed*
[2] *beautifully dressed*
[3] *at all*

O Willie was a witty wight,[4]
And had o'things an unco slight;[5]
Auld Reekie ay he keppit[6] tight,
    And trig and braw:[7]
But now they'll busk[8] her like a fright,
    Willie's awa.—

The stiffest o'them a' he bow'd,
The bauldest o'them a' he cow'd,
They durst nae mair than he allow'd
    That was a law:
We've lost a birkie weel worth gowd,[9]
    Willie's awa.—

Now gawkies, tawpies, gowks[10] and fools,
Frae colleges and boarding-schools
May sprout like simmer puddock-stools[11]
    In glen and shaw[12]
He wha could brush them down to mools[13]
    Willie's awa.—

The brethren o' the commerce-chaumer[14]
May mourn their loss wi' doolfu'[15] clamour;
He was a dictionar and grammar
    Amang them a':
I fear they'll now mak mony a stammer,
    Willie's awa.—

Nae mair we see his levee door
Philosophers and Poets pour,

---

[4] *fellow*
[5] *uncommon dexterity*
[6] *kept*
[7] *smart and fine*
[8] *dress*
[9] *a fellow well worth gold*
[10] *boobies, senseless girls, dolts*
[11] *summer toadstools*
[12] *wooded hill*
[13] *clods*
[14] *chamber of commerce*
[15] *sorrowful*

And toothy Critics by the score
   In bloody raw;
The Adjutant of a' the core
   Willie's awa.—

Now worthy Greg'ry's latin face,
Tytler's and Greenfields modest grace,
Mckenzie, Stuart* such a brace
   As Rome ne'er saw;
They a' maun[16] meet some ither place,
   Willie's awa.—

Poor BURNS—even Scotch Drink canna quicken,
He cheeps like some bewilder'd chicken,
Scar'd frae its minnie[17] and the cleckin[18]
   By hoodie-craw:[19]
Grief's gien his heart an unco kickin,
   Willie's awa.—

Now ev'ry sour-mou'd, girnin blellum,[20]
And Calvin's folk are fit to fell him;
Ilk self-conceited, critic skellum[21]
   His quill may draw;
He wha could brawlie ward their blellum
   Willie's awa.—

Up wimpling,[22] stately Tweed I've sped,
And Eden scenes on chrystal Jed,
And Ettrick banks now roaring red
   While tempests blaw;
But ev'ry joy and pleasure's fled,
   Willie's awa.—

---

* ie, Dr James Gregory (1753–1821); Alexander Fraser Tytler (1747–1813); The Reverend William Greenfield (d. 1827); Henry Mackenzie (1745–1831); and Professor Dugald Stewart (1753–1828).

[16] *all must*
[17] *mother* [18] *brood*
[19] *hooded crow*
[20] *sour-mouthed, snarling blusterer*
[21] *scoundrel*
[22] *meandering*

May I be Slander's common speech;
A text for Infamy to preach;
And lastly, streekit[23] out to bleach
   In winter snaw
When I forget thee, WILLIE CREECH,
   Tho' far awa!—

May never wicked Fortune touzle[24] him,
May never wicked men bamboozle him,
Until a pow as auld's[25] Methusalem
   He canty claw:[26]
Then to the blessed, new Jerusalem
   Fleet-wing awa.—

[*WILLIAM CREECH (1745–1815) was the uncommonly mean book-seller who subscribed and sold copies of Burns's poems. His shop was a meetingplace for scholars. Creech became a member of the Edinburgh Town Council 1780, served as a Magistrate 1788, and as Lord Provost 1811. This poem reflects the Burns–Creech relationship before they finally quarrelled over delayed payments.*]

2 MR PATISON Bookseller Paisley*

Dear Sir,
   I am sorry I was out of Edinr making a slight pilgrimage to the classic scenes of this country, when I was favored with yours of the 11th inst inclosing an order of the Paisley banking company on the Royal Bank, for twenty-two pounds, seven shillings Sterling, payment in full, after carriage deducted, for ninety copies of my book I sent you.—According to your motions, I see you will have left Scotland before this reaches you otherwise I would send you Holy Willie with all my heart.—I was so hurried that I absolutely

---

[23] *stretched*
[24] *ruffle*
[25] *head as old as*
[26] *pleasantly scratch*

* Printed in James Hogg and William Motherwell: *The Works of Robert Burns* . . . Glasgow 1834–6, 5 vols. Alexander Pattison was a Paisley manufacturer whom Burns dubbed 'bookseller' because of his success in disposing of a considerable number of copies of the first Edinburgh Edition of his poems.

forgot several things I ought to have minded, among the rest, sending books to Mr Cowan, but any orders of yours will be answered for at Creech's shop.—You will please remember that non-subscribers pay six shillings, this is Creech's profit; but those who have subscribed, though their names may have been neglected in the printed list which is very incorrect, they are supplied at the subscription price.—I was not at Glasgow, nor do I intend for London; and I think Mrs Fame is very idle to tell so many lies on a poor Poet.—When you or Mr Cowan write for copies, if you should want any, direct to Mr Hill at Mr Creech's shop, and I write to Mr Hill by this post to answer either of your orders. Hill is Mr Creech's first Clerk, and Creech himself is presently in London.—I suppose I shall have the pleasure, against your return to Paisley, of assuring you how much I am,

Dr Sir, your obliged humble servt

ROBT BURNS

Berrywell
  near Dunse
May 17th 1787

3 MR PETER HILL Care of Mr Creech, Bookseller, Edinburgh.*

Dr Sir

If Mr Alexr Pattison, or Mr Cowan from Paisley, or in general any other of these to whom I have sent copies on credit before, apply to you, you will give them what number they demand when they require it; provided always that those who are non-subscribers shall pay one shilling more than subscribers.—This I write to you when I am miserably fou, [*ie tipsy*], consequently it must be the sentiments of my heart.—

ROBERT BURNS

May 17th 1787

4 Mr PETER HILL at Mr Creech's Shop Edinr**

---

* Printed in William Scott Douglas: *The Works of Robert Burns* . . . Edinburgh 1877–9 6 vols. Peter Hill (1754–1837): After serving as Creech's clerk, Hill set up his own bookshop in 1788. He later became Edinburgh's City Treasurer and Treasurer of Heriot's Hospital.

** Printed in William Wallace: *The Life and Works of Robert Burns,* edited by Robert Chambers, revised by William Wallace . . . Edinburgh 1896, 4 vols.

Dear Sir,

Any more letters for me that may come to your care, send them to Dumfries, directed to be detained till called for.—I mean this direction only for a week; afterwards direct to me at Mossgiel, near Mauchline.—Today I set out for a ride thro' Northumberland-shire.—I beg you or Mr Creech will acquaint me whenever he returns.—

I am, Dear Sir, yours

ROBT BURNS

Berrywell

24th May 1787

P.S. I recd a bill from Mr Pattison, which he has wrote to you about.—My letter granting receipt had miscarried, but I have wrote to him again today.—

R. B.

5 MR ROBERT AINSLIE at Mr Samuel Mitchelson's W. S. Carruber's Close Edinburgh*

Mon cher Compagnon de voyage,

Here am I, a woeful wight on the banks of Tyne.—Old Mr Thos Hood has been persuaded to join our Partie, and Mr Kerr & he do very well but, alas! I dare not talk nonsense lest I lose all the little dignity I have among the sober sons of wisdom & discretion, and I have not had one hearty mouthful of laughter since that merry-melancholy moment we parted.—

Mr Sherriff tired me to death; but as my good star directed, Sir James Hall detained him on some business as he is Sir James's tenant, till near eleven at night, which time I spent with Miss—— [*sic*] till I was, in the language of the royal Voluptuary, Solomon, 'Sick of Love!' Next morning, Sir James who had been informed by the Sh[*erriffs*] of my Bardship's arrival, came to breakfast with us and carried me with him, and his charming Lady & he did me the honor to accompany me the whole forenoon through the glorious, romantic Deane of Dunglass.—I would not stay dinner; and when I returned to my horse, I found Miss—— ready equipp'd to escort me to Dunbar with the view of making a parade of me as a Sweetheart among her relations by the way & at Dunbar.—She was 'bien poudré, bien frisé' in her fine cream-colored riding clothes, mounted on an old, dun carthorse that had once been fat; a broken, old side saddle, without crupper, stirrup or girth; a bridle that in former times had had buckles, and a crooked meandring hazle

---

* Printed in Wallace; see note to Letter 4 above.

stick which might have borne a place with credit in a scrubbed besom.—In the words of the Highlandman when he saw the Deil on Shanter-hill in the shape of five swine—'My hair stood and my p—— stood, and I swat & trembled.'—Nothing could prevail with her, no distant insinuation, no broad hint would make her give over her purpose; at last vexed, disgusted, enraged, to a high degree, I pretended a fire-haste and rode so hard that she was almost shaken to pieces on old Jolly, and, to my great joy, found it convenient to stop at an uncle's house by the way: I refused to call with her, and so we quarreled & parted.—

You shall hear from me at Dumfries.—Farewell!

ROBT BURNS

Newcastle 29th May
1787

6 [JAMES JOHNSON]   [late May or early June 1787]*
. . . These lines will set to the tune better thus than as they are printed.—

To the song in the first Volume, 'Here awa there awa,' must be added this verse, the best in the song—

> '*Gin*[1] *ye meet my love, kiss her & clap*[2] *her,*
> '*And gin ye meet my love, dinna think shame:*
> '*Gin ye meet my love, kiss her and clap her,*
> '*And shew her the way to had awa hame.*'

There is room enough on the plate for it.—

For the tune of the Scotch queen, in Oswald; take the two first, and the two last stanzas of the Poem entitled, The Lament, in Burns's [*sic*] Poems; which . . .

---

* First collected J. De Lancey Ferguson: *The Letters of Robert Burns*. Oxford at the Clarendon Press, 1931, 2 vols. 'The original MS, the lower half of a foolscap page, is laid into Burns's copy of *The Caledonian Pocket Companion* by James Oswald, London 1750.'

James Johnson (*c*. 1750–1811): an Edinburgh engraver and music-seller. Publisher of *Scots Musical Museum* on which venture Burns collaborated after 1787.

[1] *If*   [2] *caress*

To daunton me—

     '*The blude red rose at yule may blaw,*[1]
     '*The simmer[2] lilies bloom in snaw,*[3]
     '*The frost may freeze the deepest the deepest* [sic] *sea*
     '*But an auld man shall never daunton[4] me,*

          Chorus—
     '*To daunton me, to daunton me,*
     '*An auld man shall never daunton me.*'—

The chorus is set to the first part of the tune, which just suits it, when *once* play'd or sung over.—

7 MR WILLIAM NICOL Master of the High School Edinburgh*

                         Carlisle 1st June 1787—or
                  I believe the 39th o'May rather

Kind, Honest-hearted Willie,

    I'm sitten down here, after seven and forty miles ridin, e'en as forjesket and forniaw'd as a forfoughten cock, to gie you some notion o'my landlowper-like stravaguin sin the sorrowfu' hour that I sheuk hands and parted wi' aulk Reekie.—

    My auld, ga'd Gleyde o' a meere has huchyall'd up hill and down brae, in Scotland and England, as teugh and birnie as a vera devil wi'me.—It's true, she's as poor's a Sang-maker and as hard's a kirk, and tipper-taipers when she taks the gate first like a Lady's gentlewoman in a minuwae, or a hen on a het girdle, but she's a yauld, poutherie Girran for a'that; and has a stomach like Willie Stalker's meere that was hae digeested tumbler-wheels, for she'll whip me off her five stimparts o' the best aits at a down-sittin and ne'er fash her thumb.—When ance her ringbanes and spavies, her crucks and cramps, are fairly soupl'd, she beets to, beets to, and ay the hindmost hour the tightest.—I could wager her price to a thretty pennies that, for twa or three wooks ridin at

---

[1] *bloom*
[2] *summer*   [3] *snow*
[4] *discourage*

* Printed in Cromek, 1808: see note to letter 1 above. William Nicol (1744–97). Classical master at the High School 1774–95. He was a man of great talent and ability, but his vanity and irascibility made him an embarrassing friend at times.

fifty mile a day, the deil-sticket a five gallopers acqueesh Clyde, and Whithorn could cast saut in her tail.—

I hae dander'd owre a' the kintra frae Dumbar to Selcraig, and hae forgather'd wi' monie a guid fallow, and monie a weelfar'd hizzie.—I met wi' twa dink quines in particlar, ane o' them a sonsie, fine fodgel lass, baith braw and bonie; the tither was a clean-shankit, straught, tight, weel-far'd winch, as blythe's a lintwhite on a flowerie thorn, and as sweet and modest's a new blawn plumrose in a hazle shaw.—They were baith bred to mainers by the beuk, and onie ane o'them has as muckle smeddum and rumblegumption as the half o' some Presbytries that you and I baith ken.—They play'd me sik a deevil of a' shavie that I daur say if my harigals were turn'd out, ye wad se twa nicks i' the heart o' me like the marks o' a kail-whittle in a castock.—

I was gaun to write you a lang pystle, but, Gude forgie me, I gat myself sae noutouriously bitchify'd the day after kail-time that I can hardly stoiter but and ben.—

My best respecks to the guidwife and a' our common friens, especiall Mr & Mrs Cruikshank and the honest Guidman o' Jock's Lodge.—

I'll be in Dumfries the morn gif the beast be to the fore and the branks bide hale.—

Gude be wi'you, Willie Amen——
ROBT BURNS

Free translation of the letter into modern English.

I am sitting here, after riding forty-seven miles. Although I am as jaded and fatigued as an exhausted cockerel, I will give you some idea of my extensive wanderings since that unhappy hour when I shook your hand for the last time and left Edinburgh.

My old flea-bitten, cross-eyed mare has hauled me up hill and down dale, in Scotland and England, but remains tough and brawny. It is true that the mare is no soft mount and totters when she first sets off like a lady's maid dancing a minuet, or a hen on a hot stove. Even so she is a sprightly horse if of an inferior breed: she has an enormous appetite and could digest carriage-wheels, indeed she soon ate her peck and a quarter of oats with no difficulty. Once her bones, spavins, limps and cramps are well flexed she canters well, with an extra burst of energy at the end of a journey. I could bet thirty pence that for endurance during a fortnight's continual riding of fifty miles a day, she would beat all the thorough-bred horses between Clyde and Whithorn, even if they had the devil at their tails.

I have roamed over all the countryside from Dunbar to Selkirk, and have met many a pleasant fellow, and many a good-looking lass. I met two neat wenches in particular: one of them was a buxom, dumpy girl, who was both gaily dressed and handsome. The other was a clean-limbed, straight, well-made, good-looking wench, as gay as a linnet in a hazel bush. They were both well mannered, and either of them would have matched in wit and wisdom many of the self-opinionated Presbyterian snobs we both know. They led me such a dance that I dare say that were my viscera to be examined, one would find their scars on my heart, as a cabbage-knife slices stalks.

My best respects to your wife and our mutual friends, especially Mr and Mrs Cruickshank and the honest man we nickname the 'Guidman o' Jock's Lodge'.

I'll be in Dumfries tomorrow if my horse is up to time and her bridle does not break.

During the period of the Border tour Burns is known to have received two letters: one dated 22 May from Mrs Catherine Stewart of Stair (d. 1818) and the other, 3 May from Dr Moore (q.v.). Mrs Stewart of Stair was 'the first person of her sex & rank that patronised his (Burns's) humble lays'. Moore's letter was probably in reply to Burns's letter of 23 April 1787.

II The Answer to the Gudewife of Wauchope House

The Guidwife of Wauchope-House, to Robert Burns, the Airshire Bard Feb 1787

My canty,[1] witty[2] rhyming ploughman,
I hafflins[3] doubt, it is na' true, man,
That ye between the stilts[4] was bred,
Wi' ploughman school'd, wi' ploughman fed.
I doubt it sair,[5] ye've drawn your knowledge
Either frae grammar school, or colledge
Guid[6] troth, your saul and body baith[7]
War' better fed, I'd gie my aith[8] . .
Than theirs, who sup sour milk and parritch,[9]
An' bummil[10] thro' the single caritch.[11]
Whaever herd the ploughman speak,
Could tell gif[12] Homer was a Greek?
He'd flee as soon upon a cudgel,
As get a single line of Virgil.
An' then sae slee[13] ye crack your jokes
O' Willie P[*it*]t and Charlie F[*o*]x.
Our great men a' sae weel[14] descrive,
An' how to gar[15] the nation thrive,

---

[1] *lively*   [2] *cheerful*
[3] *partly*
[4] *plough handles*
[5] *very much*
[6] *God's*   [7] *both your soul and body*
[8] *oath*
[9] *porridge*
[10] *And stutter,*   [11] *catechism*
[12] *whether or not*
[13] *so wittily*
[14] *all so well*
[15] *make*

Ane maist wad swear[16] ye dwalt amang them,
An' as ye saw them, sae ye sang them.
But be ye ploughman, be ye peer,
Ye are a funny'blade, I swear,
An' tho' the cauld I ill can bide,[17]
Yet twenty miles, an' mair,[18] I'd ride,
O'er moss, an' muir,[19] an' never grumble,
Tho' my auld yad[20] shou'd gae a stumble,
To crack a winter-night wi' thee,
An' hear thy sangs, an' sonnets slee.
A gid saut[21] herring, an' a cake
Wi' sic a chiel[22] a feast wad make.
I'd rather scour your rumming yill,[23]
Or eat o' cheese and bread my fill,
Than wi' dull lairds on turtle dine,
An' ferlie[24] at their wit and wine.
O, gif I kend but whare ye baide,[25]
I'd send to you a marled plaid;[26]
'Twad haud[27] your shoulders warm and braw[28],
An' douse at kirk,[29] or market shaw.
Far south, as weel as north, my lad,
A'honest Scotsmen lo'e the maud.[30]
Right wae[31] that we're sae far frae ither;[32]
Yet proud I am to ca' ye brither.[33]

Your most obed[ient]. E[lizabeth] S[cott].

[16] *One would almost swear you dwelt among*
[17] *I cannot endure the cold*
[18] *and more*
[19] *moor*
[20] *horse*
[21] *good salt*
[22] *With such a fellow*
[23] *cheap ale*
[24] *wonder*
[25] *If only I knew where you lived*
[26] *parti-coloured cloak*
[27] *It would keep*   [28] *fine*
[29] *sober enough for church*
[30] *love the shepherd's plaid*
[31] *sorry*   [32] *so far from each other*
[33] *call you brother*

To which Burns replied:

> I mind it weel in early date,
> When I was beardless, young and blate,[1]
>   An' first cou'd thresh the barn,
> Or haud a yokin at the pleugh,[2]
> An' tho' fu' foughten sair enough,[3]
>   Yet unco[4] proud to learn.
> When first amang the yellow corn
>   A man I reckon'd was;
> An' with the lave ilk[5] merry morn
>   Could rank my rig and lass
>   Still shearing and clearing
>   The tither stooked raw[6]
>   Wi clavers and haivers[7]
>   Wearing the time awa':
>
> Ev'n then a wish (I mind[8] its power)
> A wish, that to my latest hour
>   Shall strongly heave my breast;
> That I for poor auld Scotland's sake
> Some useful plan, or book could make,
>   Or sing a sang at least.
>
> The rough bur-thistle spreading wide
>   Amang the bearded bear,
> I turn'd my weeding heuk aside,
>   An' spar'd the symbol dear,
>   No nation, no station
>   My envy e'er could raise:
>   A Scot still, but blot still,
>   I knew no higher praise.

---

[1] *bashful*
[2] *manage the plough coupling*
[3] *although utterly tired*
[4] *very*
[5] *others every*
[6] *the other row of corn sheaves*
[7] *idle talk and nonsense*
[8] *remember*

But still the elements o'sang
In formless jumble, right an' wrang,
   Wild floated in my brain;
Till on that hairst[9] I said before,
My partner in the merry core,
   She rous'd the forming strain.*

I see her yet, the sonsy quean,[10]
   That lighted up my jingle;
Her pauky smile, her kittle een,[11]
   That gar't my heart-strings tingle.
      So tiched,[12] bewitched,
      I rav'd ay to mysel;[13]
      But bashing and dashing,
      I kend na[14] how to tell.

Hale to the sex, ilk guid chiel says,
Wi merry dance in winter-days,
   An' we to share in common:
The gust of 'joy, the balm of woe,
The saul o' life, the heav'n below,
   Is rapture-giving woman.

Ye surly sumphs,[15] who hate the name,
   Be mindfu' o' your mither:[16]
She, honest woman, may think shame
   That ye're connected with her.
      Ye're wae men, ye're nae men,
      That slight the lovely dears:
      To shame ye, disclaim ye,
      Ilk honest birkie[17] swears.

---

* Burns is referring here to Nellie Kirkpatrick (1760–1820) who he said first inspired him to 'Love and Poesy'. It was the custom in Burns's day for a man and a woman to stack the sheaves of corn, together: Nellie had been Burns's partner at one harvest.

[9] *harvest*
[10] *buxom lass*
[11] *sly smile, her exciting eyes*
[12] *affected*
[13] *all the time to myself*
[14] *did not know*
[15] *simpletons*
[16] *remember your mother*
[17] *Each spry and honest fellow*

For you, na bred to barn and byre,[18]
Wha sweetly tune the Scottish lyre,
    Thanks to you for your line.
The marled plaid ye kindly spare,
By me should gratefully be ware;
    'Twad please me to the Nine.

I'd be mair vauntie o' my hap,[19]
    Douse hingin o'er my curple[20]
Than ony[21] ermine ever lap,[22]
    Or proud imperial purple.
        Farewell then, lang hale then,[23]
        An' plenty be your fa':[24]
        May losses and crosses
        Ne'er at your hallan ca'.[25]

March, 1787   R. BURNS

---

[18] *cowshed*
[19] *my step would be more proud*
[20] *hanging over my buttocks*
[21] *any*   [22] *wrapped*
[23] *long may you be healthy*
[24] *fortune*
[25] *dwelling call*

III Ellibanks and Ellibraes

Robert Burns collected this old ribald song associated with Ellibanks in his *Merry Muses of Caledonia* (See: Appendix IV). But Burns was never quite satisfied with his 'touching-up' of the old folk song. As with so much of his bawdy composition, Burns had no doubt written his version of Ellibanks while under the influence: his expurgations were generally attempted in moods of remorse during a conscious-stricken hangover. A letter to Robert Ainslie dated November 1791 conveyed his troubled state of mind when tackling Ellibanks. The relevant fragment reads:

> Amid the horrors of penitence, regret, remorse, headache, nausea, and all the rest of the hounds of hell that beset a poor wretch who has been guilty of the sin of drunkeness—Can you speak peace to a troubled soul?
>
> My wife scolds me! my business torments me, and my sins come staring me in the face, every one telling the more bitter tale than his fellow. When I confess to you that even c——t has lost its power to please, you will guess something of my hell within, and all around me. I began 'ELLIBANKS AND ELLIBRAES' but the stanzas fell unenjoyed and unfinished from my listless tongue.

Ellibanks and Ellibraes,
　　My blessin's ay befa them,¹
Tho' I wish I had brunt a' my claes,²
　　The first time e'er I saw them:
Your succar³ kisses were sae sweet,
　　Deil damn me gin⁴ I ken,⁵ man,
How ye gart⁶ me lay my legs aside,
　　And lift my sark⁷ myself, man.

---

¹*always befall*
² *burnt all my clothes*
³ *sugar*
⁴ *if*　⁵ *know*
⁶ *made*
⁷ *chemise*

There's no a lass in a' the land,
  Can f——k sae weel[8] as I can;
Louse[9] down your breeks,[10] lug[11] out your wand,
  Hae ye nae mind to try, man:
For ye're the lad that wears the breeks,
  And I'm the lass that lo'es ye;
Deil rive[12] my c——t to candle-wicks,
  Gif[13] ever I refuse ye!!!

I'll clasp my arms about your neck,
  As souple[14] as an eel, jo;[15]
I'll cleek my houghs[16] about your a——e,
  As I were gaun to speel,[17] jo;
I'll cleek my houghs about your a——e,
  As I were gaun to speel jo;
And if Jock thief[18] he should slip out,
  I'll ding[19] him wi my heel, jo.

Green be the broom on Ellibraes
  And yellow be the gowan![20]
My wame it fistles ay like flaes[21]
  As I come o'er the knowe[22] man:
There I lay glowran to[23] the moon,
  Your mettle wadna daunton,[24]
For hard your hurdies hotch'd aboon,[25]
  While I below lay panting.

---

[8] *as well*
[9] *loose*   [10] *trousers*   [11] *pull*
[12] *May the Devil tear*
[13] *If*
[14] *supple*   [15] *sweetheart*
[16] *clasp my thighs*
[17] *As if I were going to climb*
[18] *penis*
[19] *knock*
[20] *daisy*
[21] *All the time my belly twitches like flies*
[22] *hill*
[23] *staring (at)*
[24] *potency could not scare me*
[25] *buttocks heaved above*

IV Tweedmouth Town

In the *Merry Muses of Caledonia* (published anonymously and undated, *c.* 1800), 'A Collection of Favourite Scots Songs, Ancient and Modern', selected for the entertainment of Burns's drinking cronies in the Crochallan Fencibles,* this song *Tweedmouth Town* appeared. It is probable that Burns collected this song in his note-book while visiting the Borders: it may be that he heard it recited at the dinner table of one of his hosts.

One of the several so-called Burns 'scholars', D. McNaught, was under the impression that *Tweedmouth Town* was an old song of English origin. But as G. Legman says,** it is much more likely to be genuinely Scottish, or at the very most, a 'Scottified' English ditty. It must be remembered too that nothing not demonstrably Scottish in origin was consciously included in the original *Merry Muses* collection.

So far no tune with the name Tweedmouth Town has come to light, but Legman further suggests that the melody for the verses entitled *Slow men of London* (included in Allan Ramsay's *Tea-Table Miscellany,* 1724–37) could be suitable as, the lines appear to be alike in 'both the metre and the essential subject'.

> Near Tweedmouth town there liv'd three maids,
>> Who used to tope¹ good ale;
> An' there likewise liv'd three wives,
>> Who often wagged their tail;²
> They often met, to tope an' chat,
>> And tell odd tales of men;
> [Cr]ying, when shall we meet again, an' again?
> [Cr]ying, when shall we meet again?

---

* *Crochallan Fencibles:* An eighteenth-century Edinburgh drinking club, which met at the Anchor-Close tavern in the High St.

** *The Merry Muses of Caledonia,* New York 1965.

¹ *tipple*
² *had sexual intercourse*

Not far from these there liv'd three widows,
  With complexions wan an' pale,
Who seldom used to tope an' bouse,[3]
  An' seldom wagged their tail.
They sigh'd, they pin'd, they grieved, they whin'd,
  An' often did complain,
Shall we, quo[4] they, ne'er sport or play
  Nor wag our tails again, an' again?

Nine northern lads with their Scots Plaids,
  By the Union, British call'd,
All nine-inch men,[5] to bousing came,
  Wi their brawny backs, I'm tald[6]
They all agreed, to cross the Tweed,
  An' ease them of their pain;
They laid them all down,
  An' they f——k'd them all round,
An' cross'd the Tweed again, an' again.

---

[3] *drink heavily*
[4] *said*
[5] *men with nine-inch penises*
[6] *told*

V Celebrating Burns's Border Tour

Written by Lammermuir poet John Hutton Browne

He often told me long ago,
    It was his father's pride,
To tell him in his thoughtful moods,
    Beside the ingle-side,
Upon the sky-line on the height,
    At merry hour of play,
The comrades slowly came in sight,
    One sunny day in May.

Across the moorland solitudes,
    The echoes of his lyre.
Caught kindred notes in Border hearts,
    And fanned them into fire.
A lull was cast upon the game,
    He smiled as he rode by,
For city laurels wreathed his brow,
    Suffused his glowing eye.

The poet lounged upon the bridge,
    And gossiped at the Inn,
He charmed the landlord at his door
    Beside the drone of linn.
The bent old man had his regard,
    The dame with staff in hand,
The careless boy, the creeping bairn,
    The customs of the land.

No fairer stream amid its woods
    Could charm the ear or eye,
With Muse he could have thrown a spell
    On the melody of Dye.
With verse upon the window-pane
    Or ditty on the rill,
His cherished name would bring us fame,
    Bring pilgrims o'er the hill.

But down the Strips, and o'er the flat,
    And up the Henley steep,
And round the bend where Snuffy Hole
    Looks o'er the hollow deep.
They rode, and at the Hardens top
    He gazed upon the Merse,
Perchance to picture smiling scene,
    In skilled unwritten verse.

Bob Ainslie lugged hi through the town,
    And up historic hill,
And through the antique causewayed street,
    Where the ages linger still.
He starred him through the rural scenes,
    By stream and rustic dell;
They felt the fervour of his soul
    In home and gay hotel.

Envoi

One sheet of foolscap, Boswell-like,
    How could a story tell;
Where was your pen, Oh! jocund youth,
    The scribe of Berrywell.

INDEX

Index

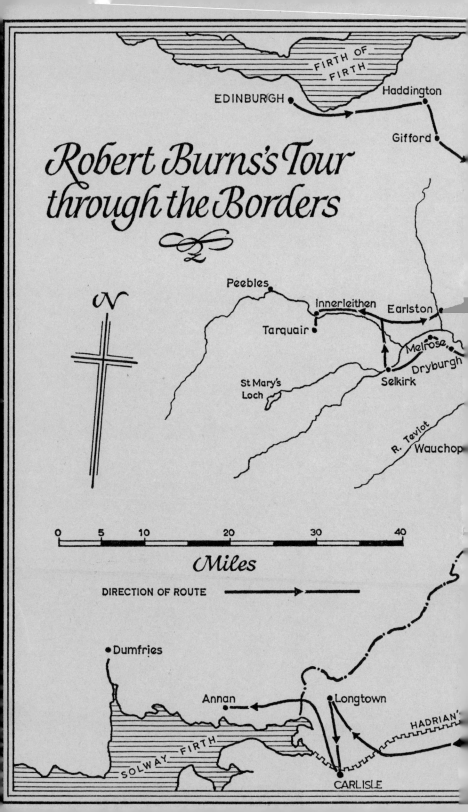